Inner Healing, Inner Peace

A Quaker Perspective

What people are saying about

Inner Healing, Inner Peace

This book is a fabulous, invaluable and unique resource. It is the distilled wisdom of many decades of living with, working and being alongside people in times and places of violence and devastation. It offers countless unforgettable stories of lives that have discovered how to transform hurt into healing. It provides profound, simple and practical activities for us to do this for ourselves. It demonstrates the spiritual underpinning of meaningful healing and peace. I highly recommend you to read this wonderful book.

Georgeanne Lamont, co-author of *Values and Visions* and founder of Caring for Care Homes

Diana and John mix their discussion with experiences great and small drawn from real life. Reading the book is like walking over stepping stones, each with a little gem for us to pick up and ponder on.

Jan Arriens, Founder of LifeLines and author of *Welcome to Hell*

Inner Healing, Inner Peace glows with the cumulative experience of two authors who have devoted their lives to the service of others, and in particular to the relief of suffering. At its heart are descriptions of fourteen practices designed to help us handle our feelings of hurt, anger, worry and pain. Anyone who has felt distress at the pressures of life will find a wealth of practical assistance here. The authors' Quaker faith illuminates every page and inspires the profusion of personal stories and practical examples that give the book so much of its heft and power. I recommend it wholeheartedly.

Geoffrey Durham, author of *The Spirit of the Quakers* and *What Do Quakers Believe?*

Richly dense and deeply nourishing, *Inner Healing, Inner Peace* speaks to mind, body and spirit. Through personal narratives that illuminate the reality that "major experiences of life have a mystery around them," the Lampens also share wonderfully accessible practices for navigating these experiences and staying grounded. In our increasingly complex and troubled world, we are invited by the Lampens to "tenderly open our hearts" to the Spirit as we encounter it in others and in ourselves. This Quaker perspective offers us new ways of being present through acts of healing, reconciliation, forgiveness, joy and in the stillness beyond words.

Deborah Shaw, former Assistant Director of Friends Center, Guilford College, North Carolina

A very helpful treasure chest of wisdom and practical advice based on lives of ministry to a hurting world.

Dwight Kimberley, Professor Emeritus of Natural Sciences, George Fox University, Oregon

This book reflects the wisdom of two Quaker friends, accumulated over many years, spanning many countries and encounters and wide reading. The practices outlined offer very helpful tips, and draw deeply from the wells of Quaker values and worship. The book explores issues around the sacredness of all life and creation without ducking the vexed question of suffering. It unpacks what peacefulness means without ignoring the challenges of peacemaking. The book will be valued in the Quaker communities and beyond.

Inderjit Bhogal, former President of the British Methodist Conference and a recipient of the World Methodist Peace Award.

Inner Healing, Inner Peace

A Quaker Perspective

John Lampen

Diana Lampen

CHRISTIAN ALTERNATIVE
BOOKS

Winchester, UK
Washington, USA

JOHN HUNT PUBLISHING

First published by Christian Alternative Books, 2023
Christian Alternative Books is an imprint of John Hunt Publishing Ltd.,
No. 3 East St., Alresford, Hampshire SO24 9EE, UK
office@jhpbooks.com
www.johnhuntpublishing.com
www.christian-alternative.com

For distributor details and how to order please visit the 'Ordering' section on our website.

Text copyright: John Lampen and Diana Lampen 2022

ISBN: 978 1 80341 368 6
978 1 80341 369 3 (ebook)
Library of Congress Control Number: 2022943880

A CIP catalogue record for this book is available from the British Library.

Design: Lapiz Digital Services

UK: Printed and bound by CPI Group (UK) Ltd, Croydon, CR0 4YY
Printed in North America by CPI GPS partners

We operate a distinctive and ethical publishing philosophy in
all areas of our business, from our global network of authors to
production and worldwide distribution.

Contents

Diana and John Lampen worked for twenty years in a therapeutic community for teenagers with emotional problems. They then taught the creative handling of conflict in schools, universities, prisons, church and Quaker communities and other settings. They lived in Northern Ireland during the Troubles, and have worked in the United Kingdom, former Yugoslavia, the former Soviet Union, South Africa, Uganda and other places. Diana is a highly qualified yoga teacher, and John has a diploma in psychotherapy. Diana wrote *Facing Death* for Quakers. John has written *Mending Hurts*; for small children *Peaceful Inside*; and for younger teenagers *The Peace Kit* and *The Worship Kit*. They belong to Stourbridge Quaker Meeting in England.

This book is dedicated to all those
who have shared their experiences and wisdom with us.
This book is your creation
and we have included as many of your stories
as we could.

Introduction

During the Russian assault on Ukraine, we have been corresponding with Ukrainian friends who work there in the Alternatives to Violence Programme. (This programme, usually known as AVP, was developed by Quakers in New York for work in prisons, and has now spread worldwide.) One of them, Alla Soroka, wrote to us, "What worries me is the torrent of rage that rises in some people. Evil has its own tools... And it's important to understand and see that... I don't want to feed on that anger. And I see this horror taking away people's values now, their faith. *It's important that we don't lose this war within us.* I hug you! And thank you from the bottom of my heart for your prayers. Keep us in the Light, it's very important, especially now."

Alla is trying to live well in an extreme situation—the city was being shelled while she wrote. But many people in Europe and North America feel that there is a war within us too between the values we want to maintain and the restlessness, anxieties, fears, failures and materialism induced by the societies we live in. This struggle takes a great deal of emotional energy, reducing our capacity to live up to cherished values. Though we're writing as Quakers, we don't mean specifically "Quaker" values (if such exist) but the universal longing for peace, love, beauty, contentment, wonder, inner freedom and a meaningful life. And we are not saying that the satisfactions which our societies offer us should all be despised and refused; simply that they can become obstacles instead of means to happiness.

This is not only a problem in what is called the "western world". In the last twenty-five years John has regularly visited and worked in village communities in Uganda. The struggles are different there, primarily against poverty and natural conditions; but there is the same aspiration to do better than just survive—to overcome violence and rivalry and achieve

1

a peaceful, co-operative community and a personal sense of harmony.

What are the sources of inner peace, and how can we tap into them? What are the obstacles to achieving it? These are universal questions; profound thinkers over thousands of years have offered guidance on them. Millenia ago the Indian sage Patanjali advised, "When a negative thought arises, replace it with a positive one." We offer a small Quaker contribution, not because we think Quakers can finally resolve problems which are a permanent feature of human experience. But there are some aspects of Quaker thought and practice which can be helpful.

Among the obstacles to tranquillity are the unhealed hurts, wounds and scars within us. These may include bereavements, problems in our immediate relationships, or memories with which one cannot come to terms. One may try not to dwell on these thoughts, but they can force themselves on one's attention, preventing people from relaxing or getting to sleep. We believe people need to find some peace within before they can respond effectively to their external problems — whether by taking action or by accepting or enduring them.

There can be persistent anxiety and pain about things happening in the world which seem impossible for us to improve, however hard we try. We do not explore such issues here, as there are books in this Quaker Quicks Series which address them. But how does it affect our feelings? Thich Nhat Hanh wrote: "Many people are aware of the world's suffering; their hearts are filled with compassion. They know what needs to be done, and they engage in political, social and environmental work to try to change things. But after a time of intense involvement, they may become discouraged if they lack the strength needed to sustain a life of action. Real strength is not in power, money or weapons, but in deep inner peace."

Our bodies and our minds have an innate drive towards health. Hippocrates, the father of modern medicine said, "The natural healing power within each of us is the greatest force in getting well", and doctors can only assist nature's processes of healing. When these work effectively, our health problems can be reduced or surmounted. But, particularly on the psychological side, many distressing symptoms can be explained as false solutions to a problem. For example, hypochondria may be a faulty attempt to get the love and attention we need.

Why do we feel that Quakers have something specific to offer here? Firstly, most Friends believe in "that of God" — something which exists in each of us, but is linked to a greater power outside us. The eighteenth-century American Quaker John Woolman whose Journal is a spiritual classic, wrote: "There is a principle which is pure, placed in the human mind, which in different places and ages hath had different names. It is, however, pure and proceeds from God. It is deep and inward, confined to no forms of religion nor excluded from any, where the heart stands in perfect sincerity."

Other great thinkers agree. Carl Jung wrote of something within us which arises of its own accord. We can speak of it in numinous terms, such as "Inner Light" and "that of God" in us — or more scientifically as "the unconscious". But he says "the unconscious" is too neutral and rational a term to stir our imaginations and describe the sense of being rescued by something beyond ourselves at a time when we know everything is not right with us, or in a sudden emergency. William James found it in every religion: "The uneasiness, reduced to its simplest terms, is a sense that there is *something wrong about us* as we naturally stand. The solution is a sense that *we are saved from the wrongness* by making proper connection with the higher powers."

Secondly, Quaker worship is a practice undertaken regularly by most Quakers which puts us in touch with this inner/outer power — and so opens us to healing. It has been described by the Quaker writer Kate McNally: "We begin this by listening to

3

God. Before we do that, we must listen *for* God. We sit in silence, trying to find stillness, to quiet the inner voices, the noise, the agitation that is the background to our daily lives. When we can do this, we sometimes feel a deepening of the silence. It becomes thicker, almost solid. We feel that we can fall into it and let it support us, wiping away the wounds and scars of daily life."

We believe these principles can be true for everyone in their daily lives. They were illustrated for us (Diana and John) in a particularly clear way by the extraordinary people we met in prisons, communities torn by violence and a children's hospice. In this book we have drawn examples from those experiences.

Wonderful things exist beyond our fears, anxieties, anger and hurts. Our friend Alla, whom we quoted earlier, wrote in the same letter, "Life has a good quality, it goes on no matter what. It's spring in Odessa, and it's very beautiful now! The birds are singing, the sun is shining, and it can't help but inspire, even during the war."

Unease and Anxiety

Our first job was in a therapeutic community for teenage boys with severe emotional problems. The principal was Fred Lennhoff, a refugee from Nazi Germany who had profound knowledge and brilliant intuition about human nature. Fifty years later we still draw on the insights he gave us. He helped his staff and the boys to develop unsuspected capacities. But he was a difficult boss. He believed that those who worked for him would give of their best if they felt the pressure of anxiety, and he was not slow to create it. Given that he had a fierce temper and was often driven by anxiety himself, the upshot was that he often ruled by fear, and many promising staff members quickly left.

With hindsight we acknowledge that there was a core of truth in his belief. Without the spur of anxiety we might neglect important things—from servicing the car to sorting out an issue with one of our children. In such cases, anxiety is like a friend who nags us but has our best interests at heart. We can learn to say with Thich Nhat Hanh, "Hello, Worry, what are you telling me now? Okay—I know—you're right!"

But anxiety is not always a friend, as we saw with Fred's temper. It can be dysfunctional and persistent, disturbing our sleep and spoiling our interactions with other people, including those we love most. It can become a habit of mind, so that as soon as one anxiety is resolved, another takes its place. It can affect the way other people see us, and even cause some of them to avoid us. Fear should be a helpful motivator, but it can easily become counterproductive if it gets out of hand.

When anxiety takes over, we have two practices to offer (the Practices are found at the end of the book). **Practice 1** arises from our experience of Quaker worship, and it also draws on Diana's experience as a teacher of yoga and relaxation, and on the wisdom of the mindfulness tradition. We shall say more about the resources contained in Quaker worship later, but this is a simple practice for you, for when you have accepted what you need to do, but you still cannot put the worry out of your mind.

Rufus Jones, an American Quaker in the last century, wrote: "Silence itself, of course, has no magic. It may be just sheer emptiness, absence of words or noise or music. It may be an occasion for slumber, or it may be a dead form. But it may be an intensified pause, a vitalised hush, a creative quiet, an actual moment of mutual and reciprocal correspondence with God." In his book *Oh God, Why?*, Gerard Hughes explains how stilling practices can be done as a form of prayer.

You may feel it's impossible for you. So here is a story to encourage you. Diana used to teach yoga and relaxation in the Bogside in Derry, Northern Ireland, during the years of violence. One evening two young women came in and asked her, "Can you get *anyone* to relax?" "I can try," she said. They replied, "You'll never manage it with us!" During the class, just before the final relaxation exercise, bursts of gunfire were heard in the street. The class members sat up and looked at each other. So Diana said, "I understand, some of you may need to go out and see what's going on. If so, it's fine to leave. But if you want to stay, we need to try extra hard to find that peacefulness which we're looking for." Over half the class stayed, including the two women. At the end of the session, these two had fallen asleep. Diana signed to the others to tiptoe out; and it was several minutes before they woke up and looked around in astonishment; "Where's everybody gone?"

Practice 2 points the opposite way. It asks you, "Have you heard clearly what these thoughts which won't go away are telling you?" Perhaps the decisions you are making will only scratch the surface of the problem? Is your active mind using a lesser worry to hide something much deeper which you need to face? Are you perhaps focussing on practical actions when you actually need to address an underlying relationship?

George Fox, the first Quaker, understood very well how we can get caught in a cycle of unproductive thoughts. He said (to paraphrase his seventeenth-century English), "If you look down at what is wrong, you will be swallowed up in it; but if you look at the Light which shows you what it is, you will understand it. You will conquer it, you will find grace and strength; and there is the first step to peace."

A number of experiences show this can work. A psychiatrist friend who often worked with anxious teenagers would advise them to keep a "worry diary", and write in it every day. Then each week they reviewed what they had written. They found that by objectifying their anxieties, putting them "out there", they could manage them. Quite often, after a few weeks, they told him, "I don't need it any more".

Karina is a Ukrainian friend of John's, to whom he taught the practice of journaling several years ago. She lived through the early months of war and is now a refugee. She tells us that she still writes in her journal, now in its fourth volume. She says it is like a friend: when she doesn't know what to write, "it knows what questions to ask me".

What we have said about anxiety is true about other feelings which can get an obsessive hold on us: anger, blame, resentment, guilt, regret. It is said that resentment is like taking a poison and hoping the other person will die. When the British authorities, for no good reason, refused a visa for a disabled Ugandan girl whom we have known all her life to come on a short visit to us, Diana was full of rage for almost a week. Eventually she took her anger into Quaker worship and looked at it in the way we have described. And the thought came to her unexpectedly but very clearly: "Anger is not a dwelling place." This was as much as to say, Of course you were furious, don't worry about it—but now it's time to move on. After a little thought, we decided to send the money we had saved for the airfares so that the girl and some friends could go on a holiday in their own country, seeing lions and giraffes, rivers and waterfalls, which they had never experienced before. In texts, emails and photos, they shared their joy and excitement with us, banishing any remaining resentment.

Diana was experiencing what we spoke of earlier as "that of God" in each of us. The early Quakers called it "the inward Teacher". They thought of it as an encounter with a personality; whereas many modern Friends prefer the less personal metaphor of "the Light", something which illuminates, shows us a way forward, and encourages growth (as in plants). These two metaphors point to the same thing which is beyond definition. (Once Diana described it to a group of Alcoholics Anonymous as "a power and a presence which some of us call 'God'". The questioner was satisfied. Later she thought she might have added, "and a guide....") Quakers believe that this is accessible to everyone, though one can shut one's heart and mind to it. John's Gospel calls it "the true Light which enlightens everyone coming to the world" (John, ch. 1, v.9). In a time of persecution George Fox spoke of the persecutor imprisoning "that of God" within himself.

We came to understand this better when working in prisons in Delaware with violent men serving very long sentences. They had all completed the Alternatives to Violence (AVP) programme, and we were astonished at the self-awareness and moral values which they had gained. AVP doesn't use theological language or religious teaching, but it does encourage participants to recognise what it calls a "transforming power" which can help and guide them in their lives. Prison was a very difficult environment for them, and some of them had set-backs, but their stories and relationships convinced us of the reality of this power.

Those prisoners taught us about anger, which had often been the cause of their crime and incarceration. One of them said, "In here, I was like an animal for about seven years. No one would come near me! Then one day the question came up in me, 'Do you want to be like this for the rest of your life?' and I knew I didn't." When we met him, he had first educated himself with correspondence courses and then persuaded the governor to let him set up an education programme in the prison (where there had been none before) which helped numerous other prisoners. He had grown into a really fine and compassionate man, and we admired him tremendously.

These prisoners explained to us that the initial response to a provocation was not anger; it was a feeling of humiliation, hurt, need or fear. This made them feel weak and vulnerable which they found hard to tolerate, so their brain flashed into anger mode, replacing the powerless feeling with a surge of strength. This enabled them to transfer the humiliation onto their opponent, who became the victim of the crime. We asked them whether there was a short time when they could have prevented this short-circuit into anger and violence. "Yes," said one, "there was a moment, but it was as thin as a cigarette paper."

This idea is helpful in our own attempts to live nonviolently. When we feel a surge of anger, we can pause and take a deep breath before retaliating, and ask, What lies beneath my anger? Is it because I'm hurting? Is there something I'm needing and not getting? Am I feeling afraid? By identifying the problem which our anger was masking, we can deal effectively with the real situation instead of letting our anger create a new problem. Ideally, we should catch ourselves while the situation is happening. But if we don't, there will be time later to use Practice 2 or a time of contemplation to analyse what happened, identify whatever is still unsolved, and learn to do better in future.

The same insights into the mechanism of anger help us when someone is angry with us. Instead of responding defensively, which may escalate into a fight, we can say, Why is this person acting like this? Are they hurting from something I did? What do they need from me at this moment? What are they afraid of? These questions help us to respond with sympathy and understanding instead of aggravating the problem.

Blaming others is another reaction which damages our relationships with them. It too can mask painful feelings which we prefer not to acknowledge, like guilt and regret. We have sometimes worked with groups to learn how blaming can cloud their judgement and, if it is mutual, prevent a problem being solved. We have an exercise we call The Blame Game. We set up an inner circle of participants pretending to be committee members of a small organisation—chairperson, treasurer, publicity officer, director of training and perhaps others. We outline a problem, such as an event which was a disaster, or a hostile attack in the press, or (for a sports club) a series of defeats. We have a card with the words "I blame it all on you because..." The aim of the game is not to be left holding the card; so each person who receives it passes it to someone else, and they must add a plausible reason for blaming them.

This is usually played with a lot of ingenuity and laughter. But they soon realise that the game can have no ending. We may point out that in Northern Ireland the blaming lasted at least thirty years. So we pause it and ask the outer circle if they can think of any way that the game can be brought to an end. The solution comes when someone says, "It's partly my fault because..." and waits to see if someone else is willing to do the same. (We have a second card with these words on it, which we can produce, which the players can ask for.) Once all or most of the group are willing to take some responsibility for the problem, they can move forward to discussing future steps. Their admissions amount to an analysis of what went wrong.

Occasionally someone may start the second stage by saying, "It's all my fault because..." But we interrupt this to point out that this is probably not true because the others are also responsible, and it would allow them to use this person as a scapegoat and not look at their own share in the problem.

It has been interesting to discover that this game works well in widely different cultures: a group of Ugandan village women under a tree, an American university class, a group of Northern Irish schoolchildren analysing the politics of their country, a British church congregation. Its principle was given practical expression in Derry on Good Friday, 1985, when four clergy of different denominations, Roman Catholic and Protestant, carried a large wooden cross through the streets to the city centre. There representatives of the two Northern Irish communities, the Irish Republic and Great Britain, mentioned specific wrongs committed by their side, and asked forgiveness from the others for their share in causing the years of violence and suffering. There was no major violence in the city in the next nine months, and many people believed it was because of this ceremony. Whether that is true or not, it did play a part in a change of attitudes that made the eventual ceasefires possible. The following year other groups did the same in Belfast, Dublin and London.

The Blame Game encourages clearer thinking, positive action and improved relationships. We will come to the more hidden issues which may lead us to blame others, such as guilt, shame and resentment in a later chapter.

We quoted Patanjali's advice, "When a negative thought arises, replace it with a positive one." In this chapter we have tried to extend this and add "When a negative energy is at work, replace it with a positive one."

Physical Pain and Distress

A Cherokee elder, speaking to Quakers at Appalachian Yearly Meeting, told us: "If I break my arm, I'll get to hospital ahead of any of you to get it fixed—but if I need healing, I go to my own people." It is an interesting distinction. Professional medical practitioners often acknowledge that there are spiritual and emotional aspects of physical healing, but many things make it hard for them to give these their attention. In the more developed parts of the world, the vast new technical resources available (and their costs), the particular skillsets they require, and the ever-growing expectation of medical assistance, deny doctors enough time to attend to their patients' less tangible needs. In poorer places, the sheer lack of doctors, resources and money, the deteriorating equipment, and the lack of training in psychology bring the same result. In some indigenous cultures, healers may be valued as highly as doctors.

Pain takes over our minds, making it hard to think about anything else. We tense up and harden ourselves, only making it worse. It frightens us, and afterwards we fear that it will return, However, there are resources which can help, using our bodies and our imaginations. John once had the privilege of accompanying two psychologists from the famous Great Ormond Street Children's Hospital in London to Belarus. They were training and supporting a young Belarussian psychology graduate to work in the leukaemia wards for Chernobyl children in Minsk. He was surprised at the simplicity of many things they taught.

For instance, children tense their muscles before a process which they expect to hurt them, such as an injection, and this makes it hurt more. So the psychologists produced small kits for blowing bubbles. Besides offering a distraction, they knew that it is very hard to tighten one's muscles while breathing out, so it made the procedure much less likely to hurt. They also taught the children to use their imaginations. They suggested each child should visualise a strong companion (a superhero, perhaps, or a guardian angel) who could hold their hand during a bout of pain to help them get through it. The psychologists told John from their clinical experience how well this could work.

It can be effective with adults too. For many years Diana has had pain from chronic arthritis. She uses exercises and visualisations from her yoga practice to help her in the same way. You might find **Practice 3** and **Practice 4** helpful in times of need. The first uses the power of breathing which we have already described; the second is an exercise of the imagination.

Of course these practices are not a cure. They can mitigate the discomfort but it will often return, and we may need to repeat them many times. Fighting pain does not help; we have to let it come, and then gently relax once more. A related technique is often taught in childbirth, where the pain can be immense. But it comes in waves, with blessed times of respite in between. When Diana was expecting our first child, a mother told her, "You mustn't fight the pain. When it comes you need to breathe out and go with it, like a surfer riding the wave."

There are many other practices and it is worth exploring which ones are most helpful for you. And of course we don't want to undervalue the importance of the medical treatment of persistent pain. It need not be done in a way which clouds the mind. Hospice palliative care transformed a situation in our family: our son-in-law was discharged from hospital in great pain because they "could do nothing more for him". After a very few days in a hospice, his pain was under control and for the last three weeks of his life he was his old self, smiling, making jokes and showing his love to his wife and children. He was able to live again up to the end, and die very peacefully. There is a spiritual dimension to this. To be as effective as possible, we need to have faith that our practices can help, as well as hope that our suffering can be eased and a gentle loving approach to ourselves.

Sufferers sometimes make their situation harder than it need be. Emotional factors can make things worse. A paralysed man was carried to Jesus to be healed. Jesus assured him that he could now stop feeling guilty. The religious leaders told Jesus he had no right to say this. Jesus then told the man to get off his stretcher, pick it up, and walk home. As the man did so, Jesus challenged his critics to explain why God would give him power to heal in one way but not the other (Mark, ch.2, v.1–12). Perhaps in this case he felt that the man's mental distress was harder to bear than the sickness.

It is not helpful to ask, "Why is this happening to me? What have I done to deserve it?" Surely this is not the way life—or God—works? "He makes the sun rise for the good and the bad, and the rain to fall on just and unjust alike," said Jesus (Matthew, ch. 5, v. 45). How often do we ask the same questions when good things happen to us? Diana keeps a "thankfulness diary" and finds something every day, even in the darkest times, to give thanks for. This helps her to develop a positive habit of mind. John once told Diana, "I will try not to become a grumpy old man", and makes an effort to keep this promise.

Two Quaker friends come to mind. Megan found it difficult to accept the problems that come to most of us as we age—the aches, the arthritis, the lessened hearing, the memory lapses. She regularly and angrily grumbled about these, as if no one else had to bear the same. We accepted her right to her feelings, but we couldn't help thinking she made things worse for herself. In contrast, Olwen endured daily pain constantly from her thirties onwards, which restricted what she could do. But we never heard her complain. She accepted it as her condition of life; staying mostly at home, she prayed constantly for those she loved and the members of her Quaker Meeting. We knew she was remembering us all every day. Indeed, one member of the Meeting who had moved far away was on the point of killing herself when she was conscious of the prayers of Olwen upholding her at that moment. She abandoned the attempt and looked for a better way out of her difficulties. Olwen taught us that a valuable and caring life is possible in the presence of continuing pain.

Sometimes there seems little chance that the physical pain will reduce. Yet some peace of mind may be possible even as it persists. Each of us once had a spell of agony during which it seemed as if we were calmly observing our bodies from a distance, almost as if it were happening to someone else. After a motorbike accident, Diana actually felt she was outside her body, watching from above as the paramedics tried to revive her. She thought she had died, and had a wonderful sense of liberation from the wounded body below. She found it hard to be called back. We cannot explain this, but we know that many people have had similar experiences, including John's mother. They suggest that the physical body is not the whole of us.

We are inspired by people who have refused to complain. Diana's godfather, George Trevelyan, had severe physical problems towards the end of his life. But he never lost his gaiety and joy for long. Whenever she asked him how he was, he replied, "Are you asking about my body or my spirit? My spirit's fine!" And there is Mary, a young hospice patient who has endured nine years of chemotherapy on and off, which has failed to prevent new tumours from starting. When we asked her how she managed to preserve such an uncomplaining attitude to life, she told us, "When I was first diagnosed, I was angry, upset and frightened. So I prayed about it, and God showed me I could choose to go on thinking like this, or I could accept it and choose joy instead." There is a radiance about her despite the times of pain and intense weariness. We find it wonderful to visit her.

Such people show us that the pain and suffering is not the whole of us. Beneath it all is something deep, pure, peaceful yet dynamic—the same mystery which we experience in a deeply gathered Quaker meeting for worship. It is this which nourishes our souls and helps us to endure and overcome. We have visited a Maori sacred place, Te Waikoropupu Springs, which symbolises this for us. There is a surface river there, tainted by salt water and flotsam; and far down beneath it there is an aquifer of completely pure water which forces itself up through the brackish stream in places. (There is a picture of it on the cover of this book.)

***

You may wonder whether Friends believe in what is called "faith healing". Today there is a wide range of opinions on spiritual healing among British Friends, from those who think that there must always be a scientific explanation (though medicine may not have found it yet) to the healing groups held in some meeting houses which practise prayer and the laying on of hands. Most Friends believe in a power which is beyond ourselves; so if we claim that we can be guided in decision-making and problem-solving by the spark of God in us, cannot the same power operate in the case of emotional and spiritual distress?

But when our Society started in the seventeenth century, Friends did not make the distinctions which we do today. Miracles, unexpected natural events, significant coincidences and providential escapes from danger were all seen as the workings of God in the world. Like the rural Ugandan communities where John works, they did not draw a clear line between physical and spiritual categories; thus the healing of spiritual blindness was as much a miracle as a physical healing, because both were divine interventions. Early Friends recorded a number of healing miracles because they believed they were reviving "primitive Christianity", and they expected that this would be accompanied by the miraculous signs that Jesus and the early Christians had produced. "He who has faith in me will do what I am doing," Jesus had said, "and he will do greater things still" (John, ch.14, v.12). Quakers and their enemies both demanded miracles as proofs.

Today, the entire medical profession acknowledges that spontaneous remissions occur, even in substantial and life-threatening physical conditions such as tumours. Should some of these be called "miracles"? We would answer that there is much that nobody understands about the connections between spirit, mind and body. Some may find it hard to accept that physical cures might have a spiritual origin, but they cannot show that there is no connection.

Of course we are uneasy when such stories are used in a superstitious or fundamentalist way as incontrovertible evidence of God answering prayers and intervening in the natural world. Few if any of the Quakers we know would assert this. When George Fox healed a crippled child in 1653, the trappings of the stereotypical faith-healer were wholly absent. He did not announce that he was trying to heal the boy and did not seem to expect a cure. There was no audience except for three young people. His treatment contained no mumbo-jumbo; he simply asked for the child to be washed clean and he then embraced and spoke to him. He did not stay to see the recovery; he only learnt of it by accident three years later.

And things happen today which challenge the limits of our understanding. One of our friends in Northern Ireland was once a terrorist killer. He later worked tirelessly to save the lives of people in danger, but he did not believe his past could ever be forgiven. He developed a life-threatening cancer, and he could not stop his drinking habits which were incompatible with his medication. One evening he told his story in great distress to a woman whose husband had been murdered during the conflict. When he discovered this, he anxiously asked the details and then said, "Mary, thank God it wasn't me!" She said, "Seamus, I wish it had been you, so I could show you that I forgive you." Each of them described this encounter to us next day in identical words, so we know it was true. What is also true is that at Seamus' next check-up, his doctor could find not a trace of the cancer, and he lived another thirty years. Such experiences do not prove the intervention of God; but they certainly warn us against being dogmatic.

And life also teaches us not to be too sure we know "what God ought to have done". When we belonged to Shrewsbury Quaker Meeting, we visited a Friend who died a few hours later. As we arrived, her young children were leaving her hospital room, having said their last goodbye. When we went in, she was immobile, connected to numerous machines, and very short of breath. John said to her, "I suppose this is the worst bit." She looked at us in surprise. Then she thought for a moment and whispered: "I suppose it looks like that from the outside. But from my side, I have never known such peace and joy as I do at the moment."

The Wounded Soul

When Mother Teresa spoke at Corrymeela Reconciliation Centre in Northern Ireland in 1981, she was given the topic: "Lead us not into temptation". But she amended this to "Lead us not into the temptation of holding on to hurt." The practical relevance of this was obvious in a country where ancient resentments had exploded into lethal violence. Holding on to hurt can destroy others—and it also does violence to ourselves. Kenneth Kaunda, once President of Zambia, wrote that "Unless we are able to forgive the enemies who cannot possibly make up to us for what they have done we go stark raving mad with bitterness and hatred". Resentment is a cancer of the emotions. Someone may want to be free of the bitterness and blaming, feeling it as a burden, but it seems as if they cannot forgive or let go.

If you feel like this (over something large or small) **Practice 5** may help you to look at what is happening to you. It can be done alone, perhaps with a sheet of paper, or in dialogue with someone you trust. It is also something you could take into a time of worship. Answer the questions as objectively as you can.

Are you feeling some resentment, with no idea how to free yourself? **Practice 6** offers a possible way in. Symbolic actions of this kind can be powerful. We offered this exercise to a woman who had many issues with her father at the time he died. She later told us how she buried the ashes of both letters and planted a rose bush there as a sign that we are not trapped in the past even by someone's death; there is always a chance for new growth.

A related practice was taught us by an American Friend, Boo Shuford. It is called the Total Truth Process, and was originally developed by Jack Canfield. It takes the form of a letter which may or may not ever be sent. Its six paragraphs open with

I'm angry that...
It hurts me when...
I am afraid that...
I'm sorry that...
I want you to...
I forgive/understand/love you for...

Guidance on how to do this effectively is available on the internet at *https://jcdotcom-files.s3.amazonaws.com/Difficult+Conver sations+PDF+Guide.pdf*. To post such a letter opens a way forward to new possibilities. But you may find that simply writing it is healing, as one of our friends discovered in a powerful way — even when sending it is impossible because the recipient is out of reach or dead.

In our work with schoolchildren we use two laminated sets of footprints, and we ask a child who has a grievance against another to stand on one set and tell the story. Then we ask them to move to the other set (telling them this will be difficult for them) and become the other child and speak from that point of view. Then the child returns to the first set to tell us in their own voice what they learnt from trying to understand the other's position. We might ask, "Did you hear yourself say anything which surprised you?" The results can be remarkable. We have a little note from two nine-year-olds which says, "Thank you for making us best friends again!"

This practice can be valuable with adults too. Once we used it while training a group of fourteen-year-olds as peer counsellors. Their teacher, Kate, a mature woman, offered to demonstrate it. We asked her to think of some resentment, large or small, which she was willing to share with the group of young people. She did this with extraordinary courage and frankness. She told the story of how she had entrusted her beloved horse to the care of a friend whose carelessness had caused the animal's death. Kate had barely spoken to her since. When she crossed to the friend's footprints, she suddenly connected with the shame the friend had felt, which had made her unable to explain or say sorry to Kate. When Kate returned to her own place, she was in tears not only for her own memories but for her friend's suffering too. Moments like that have convinced us of the value of such work.

You have the right to your feelings. Yes, they are sometimes unreasonable, and you may need a friend to point this out gently. But then you need to work through them at your own pace. It is said that time is a great healer, and there is some truth in this. Raw feelings are likely to soften with time. (If they do not, it might indicate a need for some post-traumatic stress counselling.) But it is possible, even years later, for something to trigger a return of old pain as freshly as if it were yesterday. This can be a smell or a sound, a name in a book, or a place revisited. That does not mean that you "haven't got over it". On the contrary, it is normal. If you have lost someone dear to you, it is a sign of how love persists.

There is a stigma attached to mental health issues, and many of us were brought up to believe that panic, anxiety and depression were signs of weakness rather than medical symptoms. This is entirely untrue, and if they persist it is as silly to neglect them as it would be to ignore the signs of a physical illness. When Diana reluctantly consulted our family doctor about her post-natal depression, he said, "Why on earth didn't you come sooner?" If persistent feelings are interfering with your ability to focus on tasks, or to relate to the people you love, there is professional help available—you only need to ask.

Our anger or resentment sometimes hides a need to forgive someone or be reconciled with them. There are many good books about these two processes, and we mention two in our suggestions for further reading. Desmond and Mpho Tutu give some succinct and very helpful advice which covers both needs.

Tell the story.
Name the hurt.

Forgive if you can.

Either restore or relinquish the relationship.

We see reconciliation as a transaction with someone else to restore a relationship to some degree, so that the two parties can work on their issues together, and be open to further co-operation. Often there was wrong on both sides, and each will need to make peace actively with the other. In contrast, forgiveness is a movement of heart, mind and spirit, which frees us so that the past no longer controls how we behave in future; as Hannah Arendt explained, it breaks the chain of cause and effect which links wrongdoing to revenge, and revenge to reprisal. It can free one party from resentment and the other from guilt. Diana once forgave a man who had seriously abused her as a child, when she decided (with great hesitation) to visit him in hospital at the end of his life. She didn't put her forgiveness into words but he knew why she had come. "Now I can die in peace," he told her.

Unlike reconciliation, forgiveness does not depend on the other person showing remorse for the way they have treated us, though when this happens it can help us to forgive. Indeed, it does not even need the presence of the other; we can forgive the dead for hurts they have caused. One can rightly urge two parties to be reconciled; but no one has the right to say you must forgive, except "that of God" in yourself. A Rwandan Quaker pastor told us how he was leading his congregation in prayer when he felt God was saying to him, "I'm not listening to you — I'm not even here." "Where are you, Lord?" "I'm in your house, comforting your wife after what you said to her before you came to church." He immediately told the congregation to continue the service, while he went home to ask for her forgiveness. He added that this gave him insight into the general need to forgive and be forgiven after the terrible events in his country.

For reconciliation to happen, the parties must agree broadly on what happened. Then they both admit their share of responsibility. If there are things to be put right, each of them does so; if this is impossible, they may still be able to make symbolic restitution in the form of an apology, a gift or a service. But not all wrongs can be redressed, so each of them then has to accept that they will carry any remaining burden without accusing the other anymore. Finally, they look to the future. Are there consequences which they need to sort out? How will they relate to each other in future? We don't mean to imply that this is a simple, single process. Two married couples whose marriages almost came apart after a betrayal of trust told us in almost identical words, "We had to rebuild our relationship brick by brick." We expect that a measure of forgiveness will form part of this process, but it may not be total.

Forgiving has two aspects: forgiving ourselves, and forgiving those who have wronged us. Self-forgiveness is a process (not a single action) of acknowledging the truth, taking responsibility for what we have done and learning from the experience. We can then decide to live in a more responsible and loving way, tenderly opening our hearts. In one of our AVP sessions in Delaware we two were asked by the organisers to address the subject of weeping, since one of the prisoners had reduced the two female trainers to tears and they felt they had lost their status. During our work the men admitted that each one of them had cried during the last month, usually in secret when they were in bed. We stood in a close circle, and Diana told each of them to visualise a little child in tears in front of them; she asked them to pick him up and comfort him. She then suggested that this was the wounded child inside them, who needed love and healing. Nobody's eyes were dry during this exercise.

Persistent nagging guilt and regret need to be healed. Anger is there, but as if the person were turning it on themselves. This was the problem for Seamus—he could not forgive himself. Guilt can be paralysing for people, particularly in their dealings with anyone else affected by their actions and any witnesses of what happened. It can induce a belief that they are intrinsically bad human beings. It may lead to depression. This is why self-forgiveness is as important as forgiveness.

Robin Casarjian, who works with prisoners to help and heal them, writes powerfully about both aspects of forgiving. She tells how, in her early twenties she endured a terrifying rape. But she came to forgive the man. Why? "Because I wanted to be happy and free; I didn't want to be his victim forever."

She goes on to say what forgiving another person is not. "It is *not* pretending, ignoring your true feelings, and acting like everything is just fine when it isn't... It is *not* condoning... Abuse, violence, betrayal, dishonesty, are *not* okay. Forgiveness *doesn't* mean you approve or support the behaviour which caused you pain. And it does *not* mean you should hesitate to take action to change a situation or protect yourself... like leaving a relationship, divorce, staying away from someone, filing a restraining order or other legal action... Yet even though a person has acted in a totally unacceptable way, even if you need to keep your distance, it is possible to forgive the person who has acted in these ways."

She shows us how "closure", which many people think is something people do to or for you, is better understood as a decision we make for ourselves when we are ready. This can be hard. Visualising a problem is one way of treating it more objectively and seeing new possibilities. If you might find that helpful, try **Practice 7** which is a variant of Practice 2. It asks you to make a drawing, and it doesn't matter in the least whether you are "artistic" or not. We apply it here to feelings of guilt, but it can be adapted to look at persistent fears too, anger or feelings of betrayal.

After Mary had showed Seamus that he was forgivable, his guilt at his past didn't just evaporate. So he went to see a wise priest, confessed, and asked for a really effective penance. Father Gerry told him that he should pray every day by name for every one of his victims and their families. What a tough assignment! But it made perfect sense to Seamus with his Catholic background, and gradually assuaged his guilt. Indeed, it is likely that anything less difficult would not have been so effective.

***

We haven't yet said anything about being on the receiving end of prejudice, One welcome development in recent years has been many more people speaking out in protest about their own experiences of sexual and gender harassment, racism, disrespect over disability and other kinds of prejudice. Such experiences have the effect of making the person who is targeted doubt their own worth, so that they begin to collude in their own oppression. They find it harder to speak out. If they do, it is often in an aggressive way which gets a defensive response.

When we are provoked, can we respond out of our own inner goodness instead of retaliating? There is a Muslim story about Jesus. When he was abused by some villagers, he responded by blessing them. Peter was bewildered. Jesus told him, "Everyone pays out of what he has." Think about it!

We have found that to challenge someone's behaviour, it is better to make a statement about ourselves rather than a confrontation. "Don't speak like that to me!" is likely to provoke an equally aggressive answer. "I feel bad when you speak to me like that, because it makes it sound as if I don't matter," is easier to say calmly, helps our own confidence, and has a better chance of a positive answer. We teach children to do this when they need to assert themselves to an adult, and they have found it very useful.

Bullies are often skilled at isolating their victims to prevent the reassurance that solidarity brings. Cherie Brown's training in prejudice awareness made us realise that everyone has been the object of prejudice in some form, the clever kid as well as the slow learner, the elegant as well as the gawky. She suggests the answer to prejudice is to make alliances, so that we will challenge acts of prejudice wherever we see them, even when we are not the target. Then, if our turn comes, the others will stand up for us.

We can also work to increase our own self-esteem if it has been damaged. We nourish it by success, by creativity, through the love of another person, sometimes by simple suggestion. Diana was once counselling a professional who was allowing his boss to tyrannise him. She suggested that he look in the mirror each day without fail and say in a firm voice, "You're okay!" Next time she saw him, he told her with astonishment how much difference this had made to him.

***

All our experiences leave their traces, for good and bad. Not all hurts can be healed. Some things may lie dormant for years, and then something acts as a trigger which brings a vivid flashback. When this happens, we have found that it is no good to try to suppress the memory. **Practice 8**, based on advice which a friend gave Diana, might help.

Except in the amnesia of old age, there is no way back from all we have done and suffered into a state of innocence. But living with regret and doing nothing about it is destructive. If we can come to terms with the past, it will make us wiser, stronger and more compassionate. The Swiss psychiatrist Paul Tournier once took a number of cut branches from a pile and used them as supports for a barbed wire fence. In time he found that some of the posts had rotted away. But others had taken root and put out branches and leaves. The wire had left some of these with ugly scars and distorted growth. But others were flourishing; they had grown round the wire and absorbed it into themselves, refusing to let it do harm.

Quaker Worship

We said little about Quakerism in the previous chapter; most of the suggestions there came from our work in yoga, education and psychology. But that doesn't mean our faith is irrelevant. Now it is time to look at how our tradition of unprogrammed worship underpins that work.

Quakers are more concerned with living out and encouraging the values which we share with most people the world over, than with persuading them to become Friends. These values include peace, justice, sustainability, truth, integrity, simplicity, and equality. The two of us have been unusually lucky in the number of different places and settings where we have worked. We found a strong spiritual kinship with members of other Christian denominations, Muslims, Buddhists, communists and professed atheists. We have learnt from them, and never felt we should try to convert them to our own beliefs. Yet there is a deep Quaker foundation to what we offered them. When two Bosnian Muslim colleagues stayed with us in England and worshipped in our Quaker meeting, one of them said afterwards, "We call ourselves Muslims and you call yourself Quakers—but at the level of the Spirit, we are one."

Our own beliefs have changed over time and will continue to evolve. Two things are constant. One is the way we try to live, expressed not in words but by what we do. A popular Quaker phrase is "faith into action". Friends are known for their activism, but it must be grounded in our spiritual lives for it to be lasting and effective. If we get this relation between faith and action right, the message will be evident in what we do and how we do it, rather than sermons and writings. Our founder, George Fox, said, "Let your lives preach"; and Gandhi said, "Be the change you want to see in the world."

When Friends move into action, we do not leave contemplation behind. Our decision-making processes (described elsewhere in this series) keep us in touch with our spiritual roots.

And when we join in a cause with others, it is not because we claim some special Quaker insight into what is to be done. But our good friend Rajan Naidu, an activist who worships at our own Quaker Meeting, tells us, "By joining in mass movements, people of peace can exert a tempering influence, to make sure actions are rooted in principles of nonviolence and love. They can bring principles of simplicity, peacemaking, good spirit, stillness, welcoming community and equity." Goran Bubalo was not a Friend but a Quaker Representative in our programme in former Yugoslavia *Dealing with the Past*. He wrote, "Just being aware of the support and trust we were given by some strange individuals in some faraway country who have been investing their own lives and beliefs in building peace, it has given me much more motivation, pushed me to work harder than with any previous employer, and given additional energy to all of the partner organisations and friends we have been working with."

The Quaker way of worship is the other constant for us. It has been well described by Craig Barnett.

When I sit in worship, I begin with a process of becoming aware of my breathing and posture, and the presence of others in the meeting room; letting go of thoughts and distractions to settle into a calm and receptive attitude... In some meetings, as distractions fall away for a while, I meet with powerful emotions of sadness, grief or shame that are usually buried beneath the surface. On a few precious occasions, sinking down beneath the routine thoughts and anxieties, painful emotions and regrets, I have found myself held and surrounded by a healing Presence that seems to underlie all the suffering and confusion of the world, and to unite me with the rest of the meeting and with people everywhere.

Worship is a listening process — listening to God or (if you prefer) listening to the profound wisdom in the depths of our being. We believe that this is available to everyone; if they only hear it occasionally, it is because they don't listen often or carefully enough. The Meeting for Worship is where we can practise this. We may receive comfort, peace, compassion, understanding, or a prompting to action. Of course one can worship alone, and it may seem as if sitting together in silence is not very different. But there is an added richness when we come together in worship. One of the early Friends, Isaac Penington, saw it as "a heap of fresh and burning coals warming one another as a great strength and freshness and vigour of life flows into all".

Our dear and wise friend Bill Taber wrote, "Entering into worship often feels to me somewhat like entering into a stream which, though invisible to our outward lives, feels just as real as does a stream of water when we step into it… I once thought worship was something I *do*, but for many years now it has seemed as if worship is actually a state of consciousness which I *enter*, so that I am immersed into a living, invisible stream of reality which has always been present throughout all history."

In the unprogrammed Quaker tradition, some have a strong sense of personal support, which the first Quakers identified as the "Inward Christ". Others prefer to describe the experience in a less personal way, for which the most usual metaphor is "the Light". We have already quoted Diana calling it "a Power and a Presence which some of us call God". In the creedless quiet of a Quaker Meeting, these different descriptions of an experience which is really beyond words should not cause difficulties.

Quakers do pray; but Friends are mostly uncomfortable with the type of prayer which asks God for favours. The deep wisdom to which we connect surely knows what is best in a situation much better than our calculating minds do. When faced with a problem we should wait, trusting that guidance will come. Long ago John Woolman described this experience. "I have gone forward, not as one travelling in a Road cast up and well prepared, but as a Man walking through a Miry place, in which are Stones here and there, safe to step on, but so situated, that, one Step being taken, Time is necessary to see where to step next."

Faced with suffering, Quakers hold it in the light of loving worship. Our son-in-law was dying of cancer, and we were both deeply distressed for him, our daughter, and the two children. We attended a talk by Kelsang Lobon, an English Buddhist monk, on how to detach ourselves from the worldly interests and worries which take up so much time. This didn't meet our need at that moment, but he inspired confidence, though he was a very young man. So Diana put our situation to him. He looked at us with great compassion, and said, "Yes, it's terrible, isn't it, when you have to watch those you love suffering." He paused. "Are you anxious for them?" We assented. "Of course. So now I want to ask you a very hard question: does the pain which you are both feeling help your family in any way?" Rather shocked, we admitted that it didn't. "Let me offer you a practice," he said. "Meditate in your own way for however long it takes, to bring yourselves to a place of peace inside you. Once you are peacefully there, look at their suffering and bring it into your peaceful hearts and hold it there. Then send them love and peace from your hearts. And don't just try this once. You need to do it regularly if it is to help." Kelsang thus showed us an imaginative way of obeying the Quaker injunction to "hold someone in the Light" which has often helped us since. In John's book *Peaceful Inside* for five-year-olds, he adapted this idea for them as **Practice 9**.

***

How can Quaker worship help when we are entangled in a personal problem, challenge or hurt? In 1994 Rex Ambler was pondering what was the spiritual experience which gave the early Quakers such joy and peace of mind and the courage to share it with others even when beaten and imprisoned for doing so. He suspected that hidden in their words (often so obscure to us) was a particular spiritual practice. The seventeenth century had no "how to do it" manuals, and Rex had to search in many writings; but a clear pattern emerged, which he sets out in his book *Light to Live By*. He called his discovery "Experiment with Light".

Rex identified four stages of a spiritual practice which early Friends used and described.

1. *Mind the Light.* This means stopping to consider what the Light within you shows you about what is happening in your life. Is anything causing you unease? Is there anything you need to attend to? George Fox wrote, "Your Teacher is within you, look not forth."

2. *Open your heart to the Truth.* Be honest and open with yourself and with God. Let the Truth emerge of its own accord. Don't try to evade or excuse anything that you are shown. But don't let yourself become confused or guilty.

3. *Wait in the Light.* Instead of worrying over what the Light shows you, or trying to come up with solutions, be calm and patient. The Light itself, as it reveals the Truth, is part of "that of God" which is in you. Its power can show you what you need to understand (or to do!) in order to achieve peace of mind — providing you don't lose yourself in troubled emotions. "Be cool" said Fox in his longest account of the process.

4. *Submit to the Truth.* In other words, accept what you have been shown. Fox wrote in a letter, "When you have seen what's going on in your mind, and the temptations there,

do not think but submit... You will then receive power. So, stand still in the Light, submit to it, and all the rest will quieten down or disappear." At times, the Light impels you to a necessary course of action, and then submitting means obeying it.

We use this process to contemplate the bigger problems in the world, especially the ones where we feel helpless. It may help us to adjust something in our thinking about them; it may suggest a course of action where we can make a difference, large or small.

In the experience of us and our friends, Experiment with Light can help in many different ways. As we have noted, it may show us a course of action to take. It may simply clarify a situation and alter our attitude to it—perhaps the behaviour of someone which is angering or distressing us. It may pose a question to live with for a while. It may show us that some worry or annoyance which we are feeling is not truly important. Or it may remind us that in spite of everything, we are loved and supported by a greater power than ourselves.

Think Nonviolently

Will Warren was a Quaker working for peace in Northern Ireland at great personal risk, and we once asked him how one could train for the work he was doing. He replied, "The Quaker Meeting for Worship is the only effective training in nonviolence that I have ever found." Friends have found that when what we call a "leading" becomes clear to us during our worship, we are also given the strength to take it up.

Worship does not always bring us into a state of peace. It can push us to consider adopting new attitudes, beliefs and behaviour. It can call us to change. It can challenge the violence that lurks in our thinking. Hopefully Quakers are not inclined to violent action, but violent words and even thoughts can do damage. When a little girl was disciplined at school for something she said to a friend, her grandmother told her to find a dandelion clock. They blew the seeds into the wind; then Granny said, "You collect together all those seeds, while I get our tea ready." Soon the girl came into the kitchen in tears: "Granny, I can't get them all back!" "Yes," said the grandmother, "And remember, angry words are like that. It's so easy to send them out, but so difficult to take them back again."

In Meeting for Worship or an Experiment with Light Group, we can recall our violent thoughts and feelings and hold them in the Light. We don't try to wrestle with them but simply examine them to see more clearly what's going on inside us. We then wait to discover what insights come to us in the silence. It may be something about ourselves which we have been suppressing, a hurt which needs healing or a relationship which needs attention. We may discover that Jesus' injunction to love our enemies is deeply practical advice. We are often shown what to do.

In her work with prisoners, Robin Casarjian often starts by asking them to work on the judgemental thoughts about people they do not know but might glimpse in the street or on a bus, or on a prison landing. Most of us indulge in these: "He looks grumpy!" "She's so fat!" "Can't those people keep their kids in order?" Robin suggests that this is a violent habit in our thinking, which also colours the way we think about those people we know much better. It doesn't cost much to change this habit towards others who are unknown to us, so that is a good way to practice a better habit of mind. She calls this "learning to see". She advises, "Allow yourself to see beyond their outer appearances and see instead the Self—the light. In other words, inwardly acknowledge that each person you see has a peaceful, loving and wise nature." You might act on this by saying hello and smiling as you pass them. This is not pity, it is an act of recognition and admiration, like the *namaste* greeting which means "the divine in me greets the divine in you".

We have often been told, "There are some people who can never change!" We don't believe this, and it would be impossible to prove anyway. Of course there are bad people who did not change. But that does not convince us that we should give up on others, and we can produce evidence which weighs against the idea. As one example from many, we are privileged to know Silke Maier-Witt, who was a member of a notorious German terrorist group and was eventually sent to prison for murder, attempted murder, theft and kidnapping. Before her arrest, she had begun questioning her beliefs and their consequences. She studied in prison and later qualified as a clinical psychologist. She then worked in Kosovo and North Macedonia to help women and children severely traumatised by the war. She saw this as a way of making amends. She supports peace and development projects there, and speaks out passionately against all forms of violence. She met the son of the murder victim to ask his forgiveness; he said afterwards how moved he was by her sincerity. Yet at the time when she announced and tried to justify the murder, many will have thought, "That woman can never change."

If we recognise that there is a core of goodness and love in everyone (what Quakers call "that of God" in them) our response to them will encourage them to drop their masks of toughness and indifference and be in touch with their true selves. A taxi driver once described to Diana how he arrived in England as a child without a word of English, and one teacher helped him. "It was as if he saw a light in each one of us," he said, "and helped it to burn brighter."

Robin Casarjian's practice of "learning to see" is particularly helpful to us when our first reaction arose because of another's race, nationality, religion disability or sexuality. Most of us carry residual prejudices from our upbringing and this is a good way to work on them.

Another helpful insight comes from the Myers-Briggs Type Indicator; see *https://www.myersbriggs.org/my-mbti-personality-type/mbti-basics/*. This is based on Jung's theory of personality types, positing four pairs of opposite ways in which we perceive the world, react and relate to it: extraversion—introversion; sensing—intuition; thinking—feeling; and judgement—perceiving. It claims that these combine or react with each other to shape personality types to which most of us conform, responding to situations and people in different ways. This idea is useful when a problem arises between two people who have very different ways of seeing the world or communicating about it. Understanding these differences helps us to work and live more comfortably with those who are unlike us.

It is tougher when you have difficulties with those close to you: family, friends or colleagues. But enlarging our sympathy for others can help with this too. Usually, the best advice is to work through the difficulty by talking together, perhaps with the mediation of someone who wishes you both well. There is a lot of guidance available on how to approach this. One of our favourites is *Everyone Can Win* by Helena Cornelius and Shoshana Faire.

But if you, or the other people involved, are not ready for a meeting, there are other things you can do. You might return to **Practice 9**, and this time bring the person you are at odds with into the Light, as described there. Do this regularly, and as you hold them in your heart focus on their best qualities. If a negative thought about them arises, replace it with a positive one. Don't allow yourself to indulge in thoughts of blame.

We have adapted the Footprints exercise described in Chapter 4 as **Practice 10**.

After this practice, put your writing aside for a day or two. Then look at it again. Does it suggest that a direct conversation might now be valuable? If so, make a decision at once about when and how, and suggest this to the other person (or people). The "how" can be important. When John was a headmaster, his relationship with a valued colleague somehow got out of kilter. He suggested they take a day's walk in the South Shropshire hills. They actually talked very little as they went, but the relationship was mended. And a Quaker friend told us how every time he had a dialogue about work with his Director who was also a Friend, an argument started. Eventually they decided to start every discussion with several minutes of silent Quaker worship, and then things went much better.

If you aren't ready for a conversation, do you need to look further within yourself? Does this person remind you of someone who hurt you in the past, and does this interfere with relating to them now? Is there something about them—appearance, voice, social class or ethnicity, perhaps—which triggers memories of your old hurts? If so, review your response to them and see that they do not deserve what you are putting on to them. (It is also possible that they are projecting feelings from their past onto you.)

The answer to the question, "What was my own share in this?" may be the key which unlocks the difficulty. Our Blame Game (also described in Chapter 4) is designed to show how often a problem is not entirely the responsibility of one side. Diana was once present at a retreat led by Thich Nhat Hanh, and in one session he replied to questions coming anonymously on pieces of paper from those present. One woman described in detail how her husband had cruelly betrayed her, and asked what she should now do. He replied, "You should now look into your own heart and ask what seeds of betrayal you sowed in your marriage." This shocked us all; it felt like throwing cold water in her face, but it may have been a new beginning for her.

Remember that, though the path may be tough, the goal of this work is "that your joy may be full!" (John ch.15, v.11).

***

What resources do we have if we are powerless witnesses to evil? We once attended a training in how to respond peacefully if facing violence. Jean-Baptiste Lebaubon of La Communauté de l'Arche in Southern France taught us to calm ourselves by deep slow breathing, root ourselves as a tree does, and drop our fists from the aggressive/defensive posture they may have adopted into an open-handed gesture of welcome to the potential aggressor. One of our group was very angry at this: "What if they're going to hurt you? What if they might even kill you?" Jean-Baptiste smiled; "Would you prefer to die tense or relaxed?" he asked.

But, as he then showed us, weakness need not be a passive acceptance of whatever comes at us. It can have a spiritual power of its own which challenges the force of the aggressor. Gandhi sometimes put women at the forefront of his marches when he anticipated police brutality; he knew that they were much less likely than men to respond to aggression with aggression.

Once in Northern Ireland Diana was found by the IRA in a building which they planned to use for an ambush of British soldiers. They kept her prisoner till it was over—and later apologised to her. It was agonising for her to know that a murder was planned and there was nothing she could do to stop it, except pray. But she did have a chance to speak alone to the gunman who was guarding her. She could see the fear in his eyes and felt compassion for him. She told him gently and sadly that this action would do nothing to bring a resolution of the conflict closer; it would just be one more link in the chain of tit-for-tat violence. He tried to brush this away. Then she said that she was also sorry that someone as young as him should be caught up in acts of violence. He was visibly upset.

Diana told our friend Sean what had happened. Sean had been an IRA explosives expert; later he found faith and became an active worker for the local Peace and Reconciliation Group. He said to her, "I'm not surprised that the attack misfired." She asked him to explain. He said, "We're not inhuman. Putting my old hat on, we need to be sparked on by the other person's fear or aggression. If I had encountered someone during an operation who had your peaceful attitude, I would have found it hard to carry on." Is this a clue to the story of Jesus and the woman caught in the act of adultery? (John ch.8, v.1–11). Instead of confronting the angry crowd, he crouched down to draw in the dust, and all the rage and anger just went over his head!

Even endurance is a positive stance. Nadezhda Mandelstam was the widow of a famous poet who died in Stalin's gulag. Living in exile within Russia during the last days of Stalin, she wrote,

Like nearly all women in my situation, I had a vision one night that phantom protectors had come to avenge me... But immediately, almost at the same second, I brushed it aside, deciding I did not want my own fascists. Better that all these monsters die off in their country villas, enjoying their retirement on pensions worthy of executioners. I would not want any band of killers to take vengeance on them for me. The last thing I wish is to resemble them.

And she comments on the book of memories she is writing:

Even if it is destroyed, it may not have been entirely in vain. Before being consigned to the flames, it will be read by those whose expert task it is to destroy books, to eradicate words, to stamp out thought. They will understand none of it, but perhaps somewhere in the recesses of their strange minds the idea will stick that this crazy old woman fears nothing and despises force. It will be something if they understand that.

What a powerful expression of faith in nonviolence! The acceptance of our powerlessness can bring a certain tranquillity and even joy.

Nature, Art and Time

During the two-year coronavirus pandemic, we managed to go for a walk almost every day and usually in the countryside. We were not rushing to go somewhere or get something done; so we could slow down and attend to the beauty and marvellous complexity of nature. Even what is called a weed is a miracle when one looks closely. When a Quaker friend went on a long sponsored walk years ago, his son gave him a magnifying glass. "Why do I need this?" he asked. "You'll find out," was the reply.

John Woolman travelled to England at the end of his life and was deeply distressed by much of what he saw: the grinding trade and commerce (so often connected with slavery), the dirt, the excess wealth and dire poverty, and the cruel treatment of working animals. Indeed, he refused to travel by coach when he saw how the horses were abused. So he went on foot from London to Westmoreland and then to York, very oppressed in mind. But he noted, "The sight of the innocent birds in the branches and sheep in the fields, who act according to the will of their Creator, hath seemed to mitigate my trouble." This recalls Alla Soroka's letter from a city under attack, and how she found joy in the arrival of spring.

We once had a week's training with a Zen Buddhist monk, Dai-En Bennage. She taught us to walk very slowly in the open air; whenever something caught our attention we were to stand still and contemplate it for three deep breaths, then let it go and move on. What made us pause was usually a lovely natural object; but when we noticed a piece of litter or the sound of an aeroplane, she told us not to ignore it but give it the same close attention. It was wonderful how this attentiveness calmed our minds.

There is a beautiful picture of moorland by the Quaker artist Judith Bromley Nicholls, in Friends House, London. Beneath it are some of her words: "Like many people, I suspect, I spend my life going from task to task, to entertainment and back, from one occupation to another, not allowing for any spaces in between... wide open spaces where I can just BE — be where and as I am... With a better balance between doing and being, giving and receiving, might my existence become more connected and valuable?"

But nature contributes to our anxieties too as we contemplate the ways that humankind damages our planet and threatens the lives of many species including our own. We have indicated some of the ways to turn crippling worry into energy for change. We would like to add here our conviction that nature itself has an extraordinary capacity to adapt to threat and change, as it did through the Ice Ages and the asteroid strike which destroyed the dinosaurs. Species come and go, but only extreme heat or cold could wipe out life itself. In 1980 Mount St Helens in Oregon devasted everything for miles around with an explosive eruption. When we visited it a few years later, we were astonished at how nature had regenerated in profusion, with new species which had not been there before. Whether the human species will survive catastrophe is another matter; if we do not, it will have been our own fault. This may not be a comforting conclusion, but it gives us a sense of perspective.

Of course not everything we see on our walks is beautiful. And it is sad how often what is ugly is man-made. This too can challenge us. We live in both worlds, the natural and the human. We can try to ensure that what we create and use in the man-made world is as beautiful as possible, and this will contribute to our peace of mind. Using our skills to craft something fine with a paintbrush, a chisel, a needle, a musical instrument or a computer brings many of us a feeling of tranquillity.

The creation of a work of art is a way to oppose the kingdom of darkness and death. The largest piece of community art in the world is the NAMES Project AIDS Memorial Quilt, commemorating the deaths of almost 100,000 people, and weighing an estimated 54 tons. Each panel was made by an individual or group to commemorate those they knew well or respected from afar, who died of AIDS. The fact that so many hands were involved in the making increases its value as an act of healing.

To contemplate a great work of art deeply and unhurriedly can bring us peace and healing too. In 1996, during a hectic working tour, we were able to see a unique exhibition in which twenty-one of the thirty-five known paintings of Vermeer were shown. Vermeer's themes are light and silence, which are at the heart of Quaker spirituality. He gives an aura of eternity to simple subjects such as a girl trying on a necklace or pouring a drink of milk. These paintings nourished us deeply in the busy days that followed.

They recalled a moving moment in Proust's great novel. The writer Bergotte, who is dying, sits in front of *A View of Delft*, and weighs his life's work against the care with which Vermeer had painted a small patch of yellow bricks. He reflects that the obligation we feel to do good, to be kind and thoughtful comes from a source which is mysterious,

> like the patch of yellow wall painted with so much skill and refinement by an artist destined to be for ever unknown and barely identified under the name Vermeer. All these obligations, which have no sanction in our present life, seem to belong to a different world, a world based on kindness, scrupulousness, self-sacrifice, a world entirely different from this... [they follow] those unknown laws which we obeyed because we bore their precepts in our hearts, not knowing whose hand had traced them there—those laws to which every profound work of the intellect brings us nearer.

Practice 11 helps us to look with greater attention. You will need a pencil (the softer the better) and a clean piece of paper. Artistic ability is not required!

Nature has something else to offer us besides beauty. Growing closer to it is a training in nonviolence; this is because it points us in the direction of vegetarianism, conservation, respect for animals and plants, clean air and water, and responsible methods of farming and gardening. John once came across an adder on his path, sleeping in the warm sunlight. He didn't see it as a threat. His first thought was of its beauty, the next of the "otherness" of its life. He remembered John Woolman, who "felt a care that we do not lessen that Sweetness of Life in the animal creation which the great Creator intends for them..." When we offer joy to other creatures, as dog-owners know, we find it for ourselves.

Find chances to contemplate natural wonders: a glacier, a vast waterfall, countless migrating geese coming down to land in twilight, or the ocean; or (for us) the grove of beech trees near our home, hundreds of years old, which suggests an open-air cathedral. They have a strong and awesome presence which surrounds us with peace. They seem to speak to us about our true place in time and space, and warn us not to minimise nor exaggerate the importance of our own concerns. The encounter with nature puts our personal hopes and fears into perspective. It also connects us to the concern for the sustainability of our planet and the call for climate justice.

Such experiences remind us not to hurry. The pressures and busyness of many people's lives are not good for their physical, psychological or spiritual health. Quakers have a testimony to simplify our lives, but we often fail to live up to it. For instance, our mobile phones present a challenge. We carry access to our work, our leisure activities and our colleagues, friends and family in our pockets all the time, which can distract us from what is actually around us. Walking in our beautiful local park, we notice how many parents are not responding to their little children nor enjoying their surroundings, but are totally engrossed with the phones in their hands.

We need spells of relaxation and refreshment to recharge our internal reserves; even short pauses can help. We were once advised to stop and contemplate for a minute every hour, an hour every day, and if we could, a day every week. We don't think we ever achieved that! John Wesley said that he spent an hour a day in prayer unless he was really busy—in that case he took two hours. The seventeenth-century Quaker Isaac Penington advised: "Give over thine own willing, give over thy own running, give over thine own desiring to know or be anything and sink down to the seed which God sows in the heart, and let that grow in thee and be in thee and breathe in thee and act in thee."

In one Quaker school in Pennsylvania, the small number of teachers who were Friends agreed to start all their lessons with a minute of quiet. They told the pupils to use this to put aside what they'd been doing and their thoughts about what was coming later, and prepare themselves for the immediate task. The young people found this so helpful that they asked the school to institute it for every class.

So, consider how you plan your time. Temperaments differ, and so do energy levels. John is happy to work in bursts of intense activity (such as a piece of writing or a teaching course, or a visit abroad) followed by more relaxed spells. Diana prefers a more even pace, with enough time for herself every day. What is clear to us is that we need to be gentle and understanding towards ourselves if we are to be of any use to others. Burnt-out people are of little use, and can actually cause damage. Our walks in nature have been one of our ways of looking after ourselves. Listening to music with full attention, and a daily time of worship are others.

As well as daily times of stillness, sometimes it's good to plan a longer "time out" from the rush and pressures of modern life. For some it might be a walking pilgrimage, for others a stay in a monastic community. When we were at Pendle Hill, the Quaker Center in Pennsylvania, Diana had the opportunity to take a time of silent retreat in a hut away from the crowd. She gathered her books, her journal and art materials, ready for this time on her own. On the table waiting for her was the picture of a cat asleep on a sofa and a little child, and a quotation by D.H. Lawrence:

All that matters is to be one with the living God,
to be a creature in the house of the God of life,
like a cat asleep on a chair, at peace, in peace,
and one with the master of the house, the mistress,
at home.

She didn't touch the things she had brought with her, but followed this advice. It was a wonderful discovery of how a time of "just being" can be deeply nourishing. In her moments of stillness, or during the pauses on our walks, she takes herself back to that sustaining experience, too deep to put into words.

Choose Joy

Brian Keenan and John McCarthy were held as hostages in Beirut for four and a half years. In the many times of darkness, fear, uncertainty and even torture, John consistently encouraged Brian, "Choose joy!" Is there any possibility that we can follow that advice in situations which seem unendurable? We feel humbled by the challenge of answering the question, since we don't know whether we could do it ourselves. Nonetheless, this book would be incomplete if we didn't consider it.

Choosing joy does not mean turning one's back on suffering. We have seen Desmond Tutu sitting on the floor in uncontrollable tears at the latest heartless outrage of the apartheid government in South Africa. Yet he was a man with an inexhaustible and contagious flow of gaiety and joy. Pamela Haines was grieving for a series of personal sorrows, which left her feeling disconnected from the much larger troubles in the world, such as a huge earthquake in Haiti. Then the thought came to her,

> What if I didn't have to think of all [my] troubles as my own private little pool of grief? What if I could leave my backyard and come out to the sea with everyone else who was grieving all the loss of the world... If my tears can flow in with the tears of those who lost so much in Haiti, then we can be bound together in our loss... Maybe that string of losses just loosened my share of the tears of the world... mine to feel but not to possess or control.

It is hard to give of one's best in very demanding circumstances if one is not "in training", so to speak. Gordon Wilson astonished the people of Ireland when he publicly forgave the bombers who killed his daughter and injured him at Enniskillen in 1987.

When we talked about him to a mutual friend we were told, "You wouldn't be surprised if you knew him. That's how he lived his life every day." So we should not wait for some extreme situation, but make a start today. If we can make a daily habit of cultivating peace in ourselves, we will be more prepared for bad times if they come. Thich Nhat Hanh's book *Peace Is Every Step* is the best guide we know to doing this.

Some of our friends feel overwhelmed by the amount of pain and misery across the world. Joy seems almost beyond their reach. And when we try to comprehend the injustice, the suffering, war, cruelty and oppression, the poverty, the habitual indifference of the very rich, and then add the effects of sickness and natural disasters, it can seem as though our only choice is between anger and despair.

Sometimes there is nothing more we can say or do. In a bad period during the Northern Irish troubles, a new atrocity on the news one morning was enough to send Diana into uncontrollable tears. Our friend Bidi who was staying tried to get her to talk about it, and she said, "There are no more words for it all."

We live in an age where we are offered more news, in more detail, than at any time in history, and much of it is negative — as if the public didn't really want the good news! Following unpleasant stories in considerable detail every day can have a crushing effect on our spirits; we need to ask whether we are exposing ourselves to too much. Is it sensible to watch the late-night news just before we go to bed?

Some say that the amount of good in the world must balance the wrongs. But who is able to do that calculation convincingly? And even if it were true, what comfort is that to those who are in the "valley of the shadow of death"? Ivan Karamazov spoke convincingly about this in Dostoyevsky's novel: "Listen: if all have to suffer so as to buy eternal harmony by their suffering, what have the children to do with it — tell me please? It is entirely incomprehensible why they, too, should have to buy harmony by their sufferings... And if the sufferings of children go to make up the sum of sufferings which is necessary for the purchase of truth, then I say beforehand that the entire truth is not worth such a price."

So it is natural for us all to feel despair and rage at times. But what can we do about it? We recall Kelsang Lobon asking us whether our own distress over people who are suffering is any help to them. What use can they make of our feelings? When John almost died, the nurse who was caring for him burst into tears; but in a few minutes she recovered herself and gave him the medical help which saved him. Can we, like her, first experience the grief, and then take steps to mitigate it?

To begin we might look more closely into the darkness, without letting it overwhelm us. We need to face reality and not deny it. We must avoid making judgements based on misunderstanding and prejudice. We want to understand as clearly as possible what is going on if we are to find any way to be of help. We may discover that even in the gloom we can see little gleams of light. Thich Nhat Hanh advises, "We should learn to ask what's *not* wrong, and be in touch with that."

George Fox had a vision of "an ocean of darkness and death, but an infinite ocean of light and love which flowed over the ocean of darkness". We may not feel as sure as he did that the light will overcome the darkness, but we can be sure it is there. We are not surprised that he used symbolic language. There are mysteries at the heart of both darkness and light which resist rational discussion. Meaningful symbols can speak to us with a resonance which goes beyond logic. Jung described the solution to a psychological dilemma as "an unfathomable mixture of conscious and unconscious factors, and therefore a symbol..."

We will give two examples of when we saw some light glowing in a dark place from our experience. Chernobyl was a vast disaster. You might expect a hospital ward or a hospice for the children who were dying as a result to be a gloomy place;

and we did see children in great pain in both places and listened to parents sharing their agony with us. John remembers glancing at his interpreter as he talked to one mother and seeing tears running down the young man's face. And yet we usually came away buoyed up by the courage and laughter of the children, with the little ones pulling their medication drip-stands with them as they rushed to join us in parachute games. We once helped the parents, brothers and sisters of dying children to dress them in fantastic costumes made from newspaper and tape. The whole place lit up with the energy and fun, and the families had a treasured photo afterwards.

In Bosnia we were taken to Potocari, where over seven thousand Muslim men from Srebrenica, mostly young, were murdered over a few days. Ćedo, our guide, was a Serb, a member of the community who did the killing. He explained what had been done, making no excuses. Then he pointed to a gap in the hills beyond. "The victims were promised they'd be allowed to take that path to safety—that's why they agreed to come this far." He paused. "I have a dream," he went on, "that one day I'll be able to organise a pilgrimage of Muslims and Serbs, coming together in sadness and new hope, to take the walk which was denied to those who died."

In destructive conflicts we almost always found people like Ćedo who acted out the saying, "It is better to light a candle than to curse the dark". A.E. Housman wrote:

> The troubles of our proud and angry dust
> Are from eternity, and shall not fail.
> Bear them we can, and if we can we must.
> Shoulder the sky, my lad, and drink your ale.

We appreciate this verse for the way that he acknowledges the universal and eternal nature of the darkness. He also tells us that it is bearable—which means there is a task for us to do for life to continue. Moreover, if we do what we can, it is not wrong to go on enjoying the simple gifts of life as well, like a glass of beer or a visit to a concert. We don't need to feel ashamed of taking pleasure in little things just because so many others have no joy in their lives at all.

An awareness of our good fortune may be what drives us to help and share with others. Having had two cataracts removed without charge under the British health system, Diana is glad to support charities which perform the same operation in very poor communities. Giving something back can relieve someone's burden and lighten our distress about it. We can also take action out of a sense of historical shame for what our forebears did and our awareness that our present well-being is built on colonialism and slavery in the past. But this should be a give-and-take rather than charity, which can lead to smugness and superiority.

People in very hard circumstances have amazed us by what they have shared with us. It was sometimes scarce material resources: villagers living with drought in Mozambique picked the last avocado from the tree, scoured the beach all afternoon for clams, gathered whatever they could and invited us to the party. It was sometimes a gift of the spirit: working with Roma (gypsy) children in Kosovo, a deprived and rejected community, we were nourished by their energy, curiosity and laughter. John once asked a barefoot homeless man in Zimbabwe what was his greatest wish. "I don't think I really want anything," he answered cheerfully, "I have a tarpaulin which keeps me dry, I have some clothes, I have my wife and children. I'm all right." This answer was a great gift to John.

Above all, those who light a candle in a dark place are givers—and it is wonderful when they give outsiders like us an opportunity to support them in some way. During the civil war in Bosnia and Herzegovina, our partners, Sezam, worked with children "so as to give them a secure environment to share their experiences of war atrocities and displacement with us where they could feel safe, because they had nowhere else to do this". But after the war, "our team began to feel we were all prisoners of these memories. We felt exhausted—and perhaps the children did too. We wanted to change this. We wanted to find the strength to look forwards, for ourselves and for the children. In the general collapse and loss of values we decided that the children are our future. We wanted to give them so much strength that we could believe in them as the real future of our country. In fact we wanted to change the future to one of peace." What a privilege it was to exchange ideas and experiences with their team, to give to and learn from each other! When we met such vision and energy from them, living in a desperate war-torn situation, we would have felt self-indulgent if we had given way to hopelessness.

When Friends are called to action, it doesn't mean moving away from the quietness of worship, but bringing that into the life of action. Thomas Kelly, probably the best-loved of twentieth-century Quaker writers, has this advice for us.

There is a way of ordering our mental life on more than one level at once. On one level we may be thinking, discussing, seeing, calculating, meeting all the demands of external affairs. But deep within, at a profounder level, we may also be in prayer and adoration, song and worship, and a gentle receptiveness to divine breathings.

***

We spoke of the value of symbols. This extends to symbolic actions too. We are glad when we receive an apology because it brings a sense of closure. Even apologies for huge historical wrongs are requested, accepted and appreciated. When the past cannot be undone, a symbolic act of reparation may be the only option. If Ćedo is able to arrange a march from Srebrenica through the hills, it will do nothing to bring back the dead, but it will have a huge resonance among the citizens of the region. Of course it is not enough—but nothing ever could be.

Our friend Sean, the former IRA explosives officer, phoned us late on the night of the IRA's bomb at Enniskillen on Memorial Day in 1987, which killed eleven people. He asked us to meet him at our own city's war memorial, a place more honoured by the Protestant community than his own, and to bring our two boys if we could. When we met, he asked us to light eleven tea-lights which he had brought with him. He climbed over the railings, took them from us and placed them on the steps. As we watched them, John said to him, "Sean, you told me that you know God has forgiven you for what you did in the past." "Yes," he said, "but whenever something happens like what happened today, I have to accept that it may have been done by someone I trained." So he still needed to expiate the past, just as Silke Maier-Witt has done. He did so not just through his peace work but also with this symbol of his regret, which he needed to do in front of witnesses, including children, a symbol of the future.

A symbolic gesture is like a work of art, combining form, significance and beauty. It may make no sense in practical terms. What could be crazier than Vedran Smailović playing his cello in Sarajevo? In May 1992, a line of people was queuing outside a bakery shop when Serbian shells killed twenty-two of them, including Vedran's brother. For twenty-two days, during some of the worst shelling and sniping of the siege, he returned to the place and played Albinoni's *Adagio*. He also played it in the city cemetery, a particular target for snipers. A reporter asked him if he was mad to take the risk, and he replied, "You ask me, am I crazy for playing the cello; why do you not ask if they are crazy for shelling Sarajevo?"

Art also has a consoling power. As we respond to its beauty, we encourage our inner healing and peace. John emerged from a bout of depression as a teenager by listening to Elgar's *Nimrod* variation. When Diana said to Bidi on a dark day in Northern Ireland, "There are no more words for it all" they sat together and listened to music. Diana later wrote a poem about this:

Beyond Words
In Northern Ireland
Day after day
The radio brought us news
Of yet another horror.
To survive you thickened your skin.
One morning the news was so unbearable
That I broke down and sobbed
And sobbed—years of anguish
Released at last.
The armour shed.
A guest wondered how to help me.
"No words" I said.
"There are no more words.
Just music. Let's listen together."
Was it Beethoven? Was it Dvorak?
It doesn't matter who.
The anguish, the anger, the fury, the sadness.
The being held, unmistakably.
And then the long deep silence,
Together. Beyond words.
Drained. Spent.
Ready to take up the burden
—the unbearable burden,
Shared with so many—
And journey on and on...
No clichés. No ready answers.
Just endurance and a distant, distant
Glimmer of hope.

The deep, deep closeness
In a community that shared
So much. Bound together.
Too soon for the Irish humour
Which helped us all survive.
That would come. We'd journey on,
Not alone.
But now—just the deep deep silence,
Way beyond words.

When we feel overwhelmed by the problems of the world and powerless to solve them, we think of George Fox's two oceans: the darkness and death against the light and love. When Mother Teresa was told her work of feeding the hungry in India was "a drop in the ocean" of the poverty there, she replied, "Yes; but it's a drop that would be missed!" Every time of healing, every act of kindness, every moment of joy, enlarges the ocean of light. Even the exchange of a smile with a baby adds a tiny amount of happiness to the total. Laughter is infectious. What we do may seem miniscule in a vast and unsympathetic world but, as a wise Ugandan said to John at the end of the civil war there, "Whatever is offered in love is acceptable." **Practice 12** takes you back in memory to an experience of joy.

We two have been privileged, as stories in this book show, to be in places where the needs were obvious (though it was often not obvious what we ought to do!). Other people, especially as they get older, may feel they cannot do very much, but surely all of us can do something each day on the positive side. On some days you may be optimistic, on others pessimistic, but that's not crucial. What matters is to be part of the community who are striving to hold back the forces of dark and to contribute to the increase of joy in the world. We can discover William Blake's truth:

It is right it should be so;
Man was made for joy and woe;
And when this we rightly know,
Thro' the world we safely go.

Joy and woe are woven fine,
A clothing for the soul divine.
Under every grief and pine
Runs a joy with silken twine.

The Art of Dying

We cannot love to live if we cannot bear to die.
William Penn, Quaker, 1693

Are you comfortable with the words *death* and *dying*? It is surprising how many people are not, even among the staff and helpers in the hospice where Diana used to volunteer. But the preferred phrases "passing on" or just "passing" give an odd impression that nothing has really happened. Death is the final reality of all our lives, and, surely, we should be able to talk about it openly and clearly when we need to? In the Middle Ages literate people could get a book called *Ars Moriendi* (the Art of Dying) which advised on how to die well. The recent and welcome development of "death cafés", where people drink tea, eat cake and discuss death in a relaxed and sharing way, can offer something similar today.

In Ireland it is common to go to the wake of a person one knew, and view the body. We found this strange at first, but we came to love the natural way that people gather, sit in the room with it and share tea and sandwiches, memories, tears and laughter together. The custom gives everyone, including children, a sense of the fact of death — that the dead person has gone and left their body behind. In England many people have never seen a corpse and think this would be an unpleasant experience, and that to watch a death would be even worse. This is mistaken. When our son-in-law died in a hospice, it happened that we were present with our daughter and grandchildren, aged nine and fourteen; they held his hands and were saying, "We love you" as he breathed for the last time. They said afterwards that it was not frightening in the least. We have been present at other deaths, and each time it was a privilege to be there.

If you should see someone you know die or find their body soon afterwards, in normal circumstances there is no need to rush into action. You may feel it would be better to sit down for a little time with the body to say goodbye in your own way, perhaps even making yourself a cup of tea. Being there peacefully can be a useful learning experience for you. We had an old neighbour, Mrs Pugh, who was like an extra granny for our two boys, then aged about ten and twelve. When we found her lying dead on her sitting room floor one morning, we first made the necessary phone call and then brought the boys into her house to sit around her body in Quaker silence and let them say farewell.

The use of evasive language probably relates to the fear of death. There are different types of this fear, each of which need to be thought about. There is the fear of a painful and possibly prolonged terminal illness. There is a fear of what will happen as we get older, such as failing physical power, bereavements, leaving one's home for good, memory loss and dementia, which are precursors of death. One may be aghast at the prospect of just ceasing to exist. And one may be afraid of the actual mysterious process of dying.

In Chapter 2, we looked at ways of responding to severe pain. The palliative care movement and the hospices have made enormous progress in the management of pain; but complete relief is not always possible. This raises the complex questions around assisted dying or euthanasia. Our own feelings of uncertainty about this are addressed in a Quaker collection of essays which we recommend, called *Assisted Dying: A Quaker exploration*. It explains why Quakers are not likely to come to a generally agreed view yet; and even if we could, as Harvey Gillman points out in the book, "We would need to discern how a general stance would work itself out in particular cases. That working out is always the challenge."

Though euthanasia is illegal at present in our country, decisions are still needed on whether to prolong or end treatment in particular cases. John once heard a presentation by an oncologist and a psychologist from the Bristol Royal Children's Hospital. They told the stories of two boys with cancer, both aged around twelve. Both had come through extended periods of chemotherapy, and the question was whether to try again, though the chance of success was now small. Sam wanted further treatment, while his parents felt it was unbearable both for him and them to put him through the treatment and its side-effects again. Tim said he had had enough and wanted to be allowed to die; but his parents begged the doctors to try again while there was any chance of saving him. In both cases the medical team felt it was their duty to respect the child's wishes, but it was essential to come to a decision which the whole family could accept together so they would be strong for each other through the next stage. We had a chance to reflect on this when we worked briefly in the hospice for Chernobyl children in Belarus. In many cases there will come a necessary turning point from fighting the illness to accepting and preparing for death.

But before reaching that stage, most of us will have to face the inevitable diminishments of old age. Stephen Levine, an American poet and meditation teacher, writes:

Fear has the capacity to close the mind, to motivate us compulsively. But fear also has the capacity to remind us that we have come to our edge; we are approaching unexplored territory. Its very tightness helps us to realise that the appropriate response is to let go *softly*, to acknowledge it, to enter into it, to become one with it, so as to go beyond it to whatever truth may present itself. There is no other preparation for death except opening to the present. If you are here now, you'll be there then.

We have used our Quaker worship to work on his advice. We found there were several stages: first being frightened of something which is approaching; then realising that there is no way of escape; then deciding we can let go of the fear and accept the *something*, and just possibly welcome it. We realised that we had already anticipated, lived through and emerged from major life changes. Some of these were in 1981–3, when we left the residential school which had been our workplace, community and home for twenty years, two of our children left home, we stayed for three months in an oppressive and unjust society (South Africa), and we moved from the English countryside to a city in Northern Ireland which was torn by violent conflict. These were losses which were first feared, then mourned; but they also turned out, as Stephen Levine suggests, to bring us new opportunities and joys.

People differ so much in their minds, bodies and circumstances that detailed advice on the changes awaiting us all wouldn't be much help. Major choices like moving to assisted living are likely to affect other family members, and we have seen from experience how important it is to avoid conflict when deciding, by giving everyone the chance to express a view. One of Diana's aunts developed dementia in her seventies. She had enough money to pay for suitable care, but her brother who held power of attorney would not allow any of her investments to be sold to pay for this, even though she had no descendants. She was sent to a vast mental hospital where she was bewildered and miserable. She could not make her own case for what she wanted, but there were family members who would have acted as advocates for her needs if her brother had allowed a discussion. His decision was very distressing for her, and left a legacy of ill-feeling in the family.

Even as we lose capacity, there are ways to have a fulfilling life in the present. Some of the problems will allow room for good practical choices. Dr Atul Gawande says that the best care homes are those which assist people to live in the way they want and give them as much autonomy as possible, rather than prioritising safety. We saw one which provided craft workshops, a music studio and residents' garden plots, greatly enhancing the quality of life.

Other diminishments, such as the loss of memory or mobility, will force themselves upon us without a remedy. The Quaker John Yungblut wrote of his Parkinson's disease:

> I saw that the first step for me in learning to "hallow" the progressive diminishments in store for me was a deep-going acceptance... I practised imagining acceptance of the diminishments as if they were the gift of a companion to accompany me on my way to the great diminishment, death... Treating one's diminishments as companions affords one a certain detachment from them which in turn allows one to exercise a kind of playfulness in relationship to them, to maintain a sense of humour about them.

Diana and I have realised that it is much better to accept the signs of each other's ageing with humour and tolerance than to get annoyed at them. Only with acceptance will one be able to discover the unexpected gifts alongside the difficulties. Elise Boulding was a great American Quaker scholar and a wise and generous friend, who died in 2010. A friend wrote:

> Despite some significant health issues, it was at the end of her life that she was able to fully find peace, to let go of some of the stresses and anxieties which contributed both to her periods of despair and to the rich legacy she left us of her teaching, writing and speaking. Her son Russell believes that it was Alzheimer's disease (with which she was diagnosed several years before her death) leading to her increasing cognitive decline, that finally enabled Elise to

fully experience her "heavenward reaching", to let go of her high self-expectations, and to experience her final healing and the victory she had long sought: living in "the now" of God's love.

If you have been told you only have a limited time to live, say three months, you can choose to live this creatively. Thich Nhat Hanh said, "Would you resolve to live every moment of those three months in a deep way? If you live like that, three months is a lot! You can live every moment of every day in touch with the wonders of life." Even if you are bed-ridden, you can ask, "Is there still a task for me?" For example, there may be a friend or relative who still needs your love and support. In the children's leukaemia ward in Minsk, there was a boy of eleven called Kolya, whom John will never forget. He was suffering from leukaemia and the jaundice which killed him; but he was always around to comfort another child about to undergo a painful lumbar puncture, or a parent after a distressing conversation with a doctor. He shone like a light in a place of shadows. The staff mourned him deeply, but we all felt as if he had discovered and performed the task he was born to do.

What can be said about John Donne's dread—"I have a sin of fear that when I've spun my last thread, I shall perish on the shore"? Isn't it irrational to fear a nothingness? Yet it is a real fear for some people, though it's possible to take the opposite view, like John Keats who died when he was only twenty-five. A few years earlier, as he listened to a nightingale, he wrote, "Now more than ever seems it rich to die, to cease upon the midnight with no pain..."

We think that this fear may be linked to our sense of what point our life has reached. Does it have any meaning as a whole? We suggest you take some time to think of your life as a story which you are telling, or a piece of art you are creating. **Practice 13** will help you with this. It can be done at any stage of life. We once used it in a workshop for teenagers who had lived through the siege of Sarajevo; they found it hard to talk about their maps afterwards, but they all wanted to keep them. The practice needs a large piece of paper, pencil and perhaps colours — and enough time.

Bethan was dying in the hospice in Wellington, Aotearoa/ New Zealand. Her grandchildren only knew her as an old lady, and she wanted them to be able to picture her as a girl and then woman with all her hopes and dreams, her achievements and also the mistakes she had made. She could no longer write it down, but our friend Georgeanne Lamont sat with her day after day and recorded it for her. Georgeanne told us it was wonderful to see how happy and relaxed she became as she did this. This is easier to understand if we recall Sigmund Freud's dictum that life must be lived forwards but understood backwards. By telling her story she realised it had a meaningful shape. Content with the past she could let go of life happily.

Regarding unfinished business Stephen Levine writes, "Finishing business does not necessarily mean you clear up all the particulars of a lifetime of incomplete trust and fractured relationships... [It] means that I open my heart to you, that whatever blocks my heart with resentment or fear, whatever I still want from you, is let go of and I just send love." And Jesus told us it was more urgent to complete unfinished business than to go to worship (Matthew ch.5, v.23–4).

There are relationships which can be mended and ones which can only be mourned and let go; there are events whose significance we can now recognise at last. As we deal with these, we will find our minds becoming less anxious, clearer and more peaceful. George Fox said, very near the end of his life, "Now I am clear, I am fully clear." We take this to mean that he was at peace because he knew he had completed his task on earth, as John felt that Kolya may have done. Bradley Smith wrote a journal of his dying months, and one of the last entries reads,

Strange that with so few days remaining to me, they are the most leisured and calm I have ever had. True, I don't work much, yet one might expect to be somewhat rushed in bringing his chief work—his life—to an end. I have made all the arrangements and dispositions I can think of. Yet I have time for reading—old things I've long wanted to go back to, for meditation, for setting myself in the midst of nature and half entering it, as I shall soon return to it fully.

The last fear to consider is of the actual process of death. People avoid this subject and get their information from books and films which are often untrue to life; so there are a lot of myths about it. We have spoken to many medical and hospice staff and there is general agreement that—except in the case of traumatic injury—nine out of ten deaths are gentle and untroubled. People tell of a sense of calm and comfort towards the end. John came to the brink of death from an infection, as his doctor later confirmed. He was in considerable pain, but that seemed to be far away and he felt himself wrapped in love and security. An Irish Quaker friend who was desperately ill said, "The happiness I am feeling now is way beyond anything I have experienced before. I didn't know dying would be like this. I want you to tell this to people."

There is a book called *With the End in Mind* by a palliative care specialist, Kathryn Mannix, which explains the dying process in detail and illustrates it with many individual stories, of which a few are difficult ones. We strongly recommend it. She writes:

After sitting at so many deathbeds, and accompanying the final parts of so many people's journeys, a peculiar familiarity with dying becomes a daily companion. Strangely, this is not a burden or a sadness, but a lightening of perspective and a joyful spark of hope, a consciousness that everything passes. This makes hard times slightly easier to bear, and good times immediately precious.

Years ago, Diana produced a meditation on our own dying, available at *www.hopeproject.co.uk/meditation.html*. **Practice 14** is based on it. You need a room where you will not be disturbed during the practice. You will not be able to do it with this book in hand. Unless someone is able to read it slowly to you, read it through yourself, rehearsing each stage. Then put the book aside, settle down and do the practice.

***

You may wonder if Quakers believe in life after death. Though our Society is rooted in Christianity, Friends have no agreed view nowadays, and this book is not the place to enter that discussion. Here we have concentrated on the task of bringing the life we are now living to a meaningful and beautiful end.

The major experiences of life have a mystery around them— birth, love, friendship, beauty, empathy, forgiveness, faith, suffering and most of all death. Any account of them which doesn't recognise that they are mysterious is inadequate. By mystery we mean something we cannot fully explain, something which has deep layers of meaning which we only grasp gradually, if at all. Part of the mystery of death is the way that it opens us to the possibility that life persists in other dimensions than the here-and-now, that there is more to each of us than our decaying bodies, and that our present apprehension of time is not the whole truth about it.

We hope you are glad to have shared our journey in this book, and have found the Practices valuable if you tried some of them. But we know how inadequate we are in dealing with such big questions; and even if we had much more space, we could not do justice to them. We have tried to remain aware of the element of mystery, seeing it as valuable and necessary.

So we would like to end with a personal experience which resists explanation and points towards the working of what

Quakers call "the Light". It starts with a dream which Diana recorded years ago about a dear friend from Northern Ireland, Paul McCallion, with whom she had often arranged seaside holiday weeks for families as an escape from the Troubles. She was in the USA then, and he had been hospitalised with terminal cancer in Ulster.

> I woke at 5.45 am after a very vivid dream about Paul; it seemed he had died and all the family were round the bed when he opened his eyes and looked round us all and was able to express his love to each of us. To me he said, "We've shared so much—it's good to have been friends—I love you!" The thing that was overwhelming was his joy—it just overflowed to us all. He reminded us that he was on a journey and would have to move on; but that we mustn't be sad. We should share in his immense joy and let him go on to complete his journey. The dream left me a little sad and at the same time inexpressibly full of joy.
>
> So I phoned his wife, Jean, in Derry, wondering if he had died. In response to my telling her of the dream, she said, "That's just what has happened! Last week he had to be in hospital as he was incontinent in both ways and in great pain. He was shouting and delirious. But one day he said quite quietly, 'Jean, you know I am on a journey, and you must set me free to go on to the end—and you know it will end in joy, don't you?' But this morning they sent him home for a break and he's sitting in the next room and he's just as you describe from your dream. He's very loving and full of joy. It's beautiful."
>
> It's hard to be earthbound today. I'm full of a singing elation.

Paul died not long after he went back into hospital. We hope that our own remaining lives and deaths can be as full of joy and love as his was.

The Practices

- Practice 1. *Either find a place where you can be quiet and undisturbed, or join a group such as a Quaker Meeting which is silent. Now be aware of the tension in your body, and for a moment increase the tension in your muscles and then go through the body, area by area, releasing the tension till you are physically relaxed.*

  Now tune in to your breathing. At first just watch it rise and fall; and then gradually slow it to a gentle pace, and in your mind, say IN with each in-breath and OUT with each out-breath. Keep doing this and if your mind wanders from the breathing, just bring it back. (This gets easier with practice.)

  Some people find it helps to count the exhalations up to five or ten and then start counting again, others like to use words such as BE on the in-breath, STILL on the out-breath—or words of their own choosing. As this practice brings you into a state of stillness you will find you don't need to do that anymore.

  Enjoy the respite this gives you. When it's time to return to the here-and-now, gradually breathe more deeply, maybe stretch or yawn, open your eyes and come back. Hopefully, you will continue to feel more peaceful.

- Practice 2. *Relax yourself in the same way as suggested above, somewhere where you won't be disturbed or interrupted. Turn off your mobile phone! Try to find a peaceful space within you. Some people may visualise this as a relaxing room, or as a secluded spot in natural surroundings.*

  Then, in your mind, bring your worry into the space. Don't take it inside you, where it will start to torment you once more. Set it down in front of you, as it were, and consider it from the outside. Don't rush! There it is, just look at it.

  Then ask yourself, What is this thing? But don't try to answer yourself. Wait in that tranquil space and see whether your question answers itself. If an answer comes, accept it, however strange or unexpected it is.

Don't break off this practice too quickly. Stay with it for a time, and return to it again if the message is not entirely clear. If you are shown a first step, take it without worrying what the next one may be.

- *Practice 3. Make yourself as comfortable as you can. You may think it would be impossible at the moment, but make a start. Fill your lungs with air, then let it out steadily in a long exhale. Take control of your breath and deliberately slow it down; see how long you can make the out-breath last. You will probably find it helps to make a long humming sound as you breathe out, and continue till it dies away. You will find that this does have the effect of calming you. Repeat this, until you are aware that the pain is less, even between the breaths. Then progressively release the tension in each part of your body in turn during an out-breath.*

  When doing this, you can decide to visualise breathing in as your way of drawing in healing energy, and breathing out as directing this energy towards the part of you that is hurting.

- *Practice 4. Focus on the place where you have pain. Picture the painful tension around it as a tight fist which is gripping and squeezing it. Now imagine your healing energy flowing around that grip, encouraging the fist to relax its fingers, so that the painful part is no longer held as in a vice. Let go of your fear. If the tension returns, accept that this is natural and let the fist relax again as you direct your energy gently over and around it. You can think of this like a warm and comforting massage, which the healing breath will provide for as long as it is needed.*

- Practice 5. *First recall the memory of what created this burden of the past and look at the feelings it still inspires in you.*
  Now ask yourself, what would you lose if you could give them all up? (Possibly the sense of being in the right? Of having someone else to blame? Of being the innocent victim?)
  What would you gain if you could give it up? (Perhaps a renewed relationship? A more peaceful mind? A sense of fresh possibilities?)
  Make two lists. When you balance the losses against the gains, which is more attractive? What will you do now?

- Practice 6. *Write down your angry feelings about the past as if you were telling them to the person or people you feel bitter towards. Don't mince your words; tell it all just as you feel it. Don't try to spare their feelings or be nice. When you have finished, read what you have written and then find a way to destroy it — such as shredding it or burning it.*
  Now you have put your anger aside, try to think about the other person with whatever love and understanding you can find for them. Then take a new piece of paper and write to them about what happened, explaining why you were distressed. You wish them to understand why it mattered so much. This time avoid accusing, blaming or demeaning language. Put this new letter by for a while and then read it again. You may find it is a draft of something you would like to send them, or it may just be something for your own use.

- Practice 7. *Take a large piece of paper, some markers or wax crayons, and a pen. In the centre draw a circle about four inches (10cm) across in any colour. This represents yourself. Somewhere inside it, draw a small black shape to stand for the event which you feel guilty about. Colour red the space between the shape and the circle which stands for you. This represents the force which is oppressing you inside, the anger and shame.*

Look at what you have drawn. Recall the saying, "The past is history, the future is a mystery; all we have is the gift of now—which is why we call it the present." The black shape is in the past, so we cannot change it. Outside the circle the future is a blank. The red area is energy which exists in the present. It could burst into the future in a positive and creative way; but just now it is all focussed on the past. Ask yourself: what possibilities does the future hold?

When you have looked for a while, take your pen and write something you hope for outside the circle. It might be something big or small, related to the past event or not. Write another one—and another. Among these you may be able to put some direct acts of restitution. The more ideas you add, the easier this becomes. Pause again and look at them.

Now make a decision: where will you direct your energy, to which of your hopes or opportunities? Take a crayon or marker and draw a plume of energy flowing towards it out of the circle. (You might like to change its colour as you draw it.) You could do this with a second hope, but don't undertake too many at this point.

Look at your picture again for a few minutes. Then beside the plume write "The first step is to..." and add a day or a date. Keep it where you can see it each day.

- *Practice 8. Choose a time and place where you feel comfortable. It may be helpful to do this, as we once did, with a trusted friend.*

  Recall the memory in detail, difficult as this will be, and visualise the details. Then at the point where the hurt occurred, rewrite the rest of the story. For instance, if someone was very uncaring, imagine them behaving to you in a loving and supportive way.

  Store the new possibility in your memory alongside the other.

- Practice 9. *Imagine a room full of warm golden light. You can think of it being in front of you or even inside you.*
  Think of somebody you love there in the room, shining in the beautiful light. Think of them in a loving happy way. Is there something you can do to help them or make them feel good? Keep them in the room. Don't hurry. When you are ready, let them leave the room. Then you may want to let someone else come in.

- Practice 10. *Recall two incidents from your experiences of this person, one which upset or annoyed you and another which shows them at their best. Note them down in a few words, and then describe at more length how you felt or reacted to each.*
  Read what you have just written. And now try to put yourself in their position. You might like to take a different-coloured pen, or use italic on your computer. In their voice, write down what you think might be their thoughts about the same situations and how they saw them.
  Again, pause and read it. Now in your own voice and pen respond to theirs, looking for a way to move this dialogue in a positive direction.
  Add further alternating paragraphs until you feel the imaginary dialogue has come to a proper ending.

- Practice 11. *Take a plant or flower and put it in front of you. Breathe deeply and contemplate it. Relax your fingers, wrist and arm.*
  After a time, draw a soft, straight vertical or horizontal line which corresponds to part of what you are seeing. Pause, then slowly add other lines which represent other directions in the plant you are looking at. These will run in different directions. Where your lines cross each other, make one darker to show which one lies on top of the other or is nearer to you.
  Keep pausing and looking at the pattern which you are building up. It is not a picture of what you are seeing, but it has the same

shapes and rhythms. If you like, you can add gentle shading in places which you think need to be darker. Pause after every time that you add something, then look at the whole again.

When you are satisfied with what you have done, give your picture a name.

- Practice 12. *When we were taught to write essays, we were encouraged to organise our thoughts and make a structured plan. We were also told to be careful about spelling, punctuation and grammar. In this exercise forget all those rules! Once you start writing, let your thoughts flow through your pen in a continuous stream. Don't stop to plan or criticise, just keep writing.*

  Set the timer to fifteen minutes, or note the time on the clock. The prompt for your writing is "A time when I felt joy". Take a moment to remember, and as soon as a memory comes, start writing. Keep going! When the timer pings, or the clock says the fifteen minutes is up, you can continue for not more than a minute to bring your writing to a close.

  Enjoy the result and the memory it records.

- Practice 13. *Draw a line across or down your paper which represents your life. Take plenty of time for this. It may curve to and fro either in a random way or to show highs and lows in your life. Many people like to think of their line as a river, or a road along which their life has moved. Mark in some important dates, some significant personal and family events, the names of people important in particular periods, but without giving details. (You know why each thing was meaningful to you.) You can use colours to highlight times of especial difficulty, sorrow or happiness.*

  Pause and look at what you have drawn. Does your picture make sense? Do you feel it is complete or incomplete? Is there still work you need to do before you die?

- *There may be times, events, achievements which need to be celebrated.*
- *There may be people you have lost touch with, and want to try to reconnect with them.*
- *You may have unfinished business with some people, which needs to be resolved to complete the pattern of your life.*
- *There may be things you would like to record for your family or other people.*
- *Do you want to say farewell, sadly and gratefully, to some people, places or things?*

Now look at the whole picture again. Then ask yourself, "Is there anything this is telling me to do?"

- Practice 14. Please note you will not be able to do this with the book in hand. Unless someone is able to read it slowly to you, read it through yourself, rehearsing each stage. Then put the book aside, settle down and do the practice.

Sit in a comfortable chair, with your back well supported and both feet flat on the floor. Or lie on your back on a fairly firm surface. Make sure you are relaxed and comfortable.

Tense your muscles and then relax them through the body. Focus on the ebb and flow of your breath, without trying to control it. Just let it come and go and be aware of its natural rhythm. When thoughts come into your mind, just let them drift away with the flow like bubbles.

Let each in-breath fill you with peace. With each out-breath, breathe out all negative feelings. Think of each breath as if it were your last—without another to follow. Enjoy it to the full. It is a letting go of life, moving easily into death with full acceptance. Feel the peace in your heart and body as you do this. Die gently into the light, not holding onto what you are leaving behind. No fear, no clinging, no longing. Let go easily of the body's heaviness as if you are floating free. Become one with the light. Become free.

When you are ready, begin to watch each breath again as if it were approaching from far away and entering your body — like the first breath of life. A fresh start — God's new creation. Gradually become aware again of the sensations in your body. Breathe new life into each body cell, vibrant, here and now. Let your breathing become deeper and stronger, energising you. Open your eyes, and gently stir parts of your body before having a lovely long stretch and coming back to the present moment.

References and Further Reading

Introduction. Thich Nhat Hanh: *Peace is Every Step* (Bantam, 1992) p. 99. John Woolman: "On the Keeping of Slaves" in Phillips Moulton: *The Journal and Major Essays of John Woolman* (Friends United Press, 1971), p. 236. Carl Jung: *Memories, Dreams, Reflections* (Collins, 1967), p. 368–9. William James: *The Varieties of Religious Experience* (Folio Society, 2008) p. 432. Kate McNally: *A Simple Faith in a Complicated World* (Quaker Quicks, 2023).

Other Quaker Quicks which look at how we can live in confusing times include Pamela Haines: *Money and Soul*; J. Brent Bill: *Hope and Witness in Dangerous Times*; Craig Barnett: *The Guided Life*; Tim Gee: *Why I Am a Pacifist*.

Unease and anxiety. The original quotation which we have paraphrased comes in his letter to Lady Claypole in John Nickalls (ed.) *The Journal of George Fox* (Religious Society of Friends, 1975) p. 346.

For using a stilling process as prayer, see Gerard W. Hughes: *Oh God, Why?* (Bible Reading Fellowship, 1993) pp. 38–9. The training John gave in journaling was based on Ira Progoff: *At a Journal Workshop* (Tarcher, 1992). Joanna Godfrey Wood: *In Search of Stillness* (Quaker Quicks, 2021) contains an excellent series of meditations for peace and healing.

Physical pain and distress. George Fox's healing of the child can be found in John Nickalls (ed.) *The Journal of George Fox*, pp. 169–70. There is a fuller discussion of the episode in John Lampen: *A Letter from James* Chapter 1 (Hope Project e-book, available free at www.hopeproject.co.uk/publications). For a medical discussion of miracles, see Dr Patrick Theiller's article in *Catholic Medical Quarterly*. May 2006.

We have found the chapter and meditations on "Working with pain" in Stephen Levine: *Who Dies?* (Anchor Books, 1982) particularly valuable. Henri Nouwen: *The Wounded Healer* (Image Books, 1979) is helpful too.

The wounded soul. Kenneth Kaunda and Colin Morris: *Kaunda on Violence* (Collins, 1980) p. 181. Desmond and Mpho Tutu: *The Book of Forgiving* (HarperOne, 2014) pp. 67ff; this book is short, clear and helpful in many ways. Fyodor Dostoyevsky: *The Brothers Karamazov* (1880) Book 5 §4 "Rebellion". Robin Casarjian: *Houses of Healing* (Lionheart Press, 1995) ch.13. Jarif Khalidi: *The Muslim Jesus* (Harvard U.P., 2001) §80.

Hannah Arendt's discussion of forgiveness is in *The Human Condition* (Doubleday, 1959). Michael Henderson: *Forgiveness* (Book Partners, 1999) contains moving examples of it.

Quaker worship. "Dealing with the Past" is chronicled in Anne Bennett: *To Trust a Spark* (Post Yugoslav Peace Link, 2016). Craig Barnett: *The Guided Life* (Quaker Quicks, 2019) pp. 9–10. William Taber: *Four Doors to Worship* (Pendle Hill Pamphlet 306, 1992) p. 5. John Woolman's "miry place" is in *The Life and Travels of John Woolman* (Philadelphia, 1774) p. 243, but is not included in some modern editions. Rajan Naidu: "In on the act" in *The Friend*, 17.6.2022, p. 14.

James McCarthy's *Listening as Quaker Practice* (The Kindlers, 2021) offers a Quaker parallel with listening in personal and social situations. Rex Ambler's *Light to Live By* (Quaker Books, 2018) describes the origins and practice of Experiment with

Light. There is a fuller account of it in John Lampen's *Seeing, Hearing, Knowing* (Sessions of York, 2008).

Think Nonviolently. John Lampen: *Will Warren: a scrapbook* (Quaker Home Service, 1983) p. 36. Robin Casarjian: *Houses of Healing* ch.7. Helena Cornelius and Shoshana Faire: *Everyone Can Win* (Simon & Schuster, 1989). Nadezda Mandelstam: *Hope Abandoned* (Penguin, 1974) pp. 689, 691.

Art, Nature and Time. Phillips Moulton: *The Journal and Major Essays of John Woolman*—"birds and sheep", p. 185; "sweetness of life", p.179. Marcel Proust: *In Search of Lost Time: The Prisoner* (Penguin, 2003) pp. 165ff. Practice 12 is based on Heather C. Williams: *Drawing as a Sacred Activity* (New World Library, 2002). Isaac Penington is quoted in *Quaker Faith & Practice* (Britain Yearly Meeting, 2009) §26.70.

Sister Wendy Beckett: *Sister Wendy's Book of Meditations* (Dorling Kindersley, 1998) offers a series of brief and profound meditations on works of art.

Choose Joy. Brian Keenan: *An Evil Cradling* (Hutchinson, 1991). Pamela Haines: *That Clear and Certain Sound* (Quaker Quicks, 2020) pp. 19–20. Thich Nhat Hanh: *Peace is Every Step* p.99. Carl Jung: *Memories, Dreams, Reflections* p. 367. Sezam tell their story in *No Alternative? Nonviolent responses to repressive regimes* (edited by John Lampen: Sessions of York, 2000). Thomas Kelly: *A Testament of Devotion* (Quaker Home Service, 1979) p. 32. For Vedran Smailović see *People Building Peace Vol. II*, (Lynne Riener, 2005) pp. 301–3. William Blake in *Auguries of Innocence.*

We strongly recommend *The Book of Joy* (Cornerstone, 2016), a book of conversations between Desmond Tutu and the Dalai Lama.

The art of dying. Willian Penn is quoted in *Quaker Faith & Practice* (Britain Yearly Meeting, 2009) §22.95. *Assisted Dying: A Quaker exploration* (Leeds Area Quaker Meeting, 2016) p. 25. Stephen Levine: *Who Dies?* (Anchor Books, 1982) pp. 73,123. John Yungblut: *On Hallowing One's Diminishments* (Pendle Hill Pamphlet 292, 1990) p. 6. Mary Lee Morrison: "Remembering Elise Boulding" in *Friends Journal,* December 2011, pp. 18ff. Kathryn Mannix: *With the End in Mind* (William Collins, 2017) p. 323. Atul Gawande: *Being Mortal* (Metropolitan, 2014) ch.4.

Stephen Levine's *A Year to Live* (Bell Tower, 1997) is a year-long programme of intensely practical strategies and powerful guided meditations on preparing for our own death.

THE NEW OPEN SPACES

Throughout the two thousand years of Christian tradition
there have been, and still are, groups and individuals that
exist in the margins and upon the edge of faith. But in
Christianity's contrapuntal history it has often been these
outcasts and pioneers that have forged contemporary
orthodoxy out of former radicalism as belief evolves to engage
with and encompass the ever-changing social and scientific
realities. Real faith lies not in the comfortable certainties of
the Orthodox, but somewhere in a half-glimpsed hinterland
on the dirt track to Emmaus, where the Death of God meets
the Resurrection, where the supernatural Christ meets the
historical Jesus, and where the revolution liberates both the
oppressed and the oppressors.

Welcome to Christian Alternative... a space at the edge where
the light shines through.
If you have enjoyed this book, why not tell other readers by
posting a review on your preferred book site.

Recent bestsellers from Christian Alternative are:

Bread Not Stones
The Autobiography of An Eventful
Life Una Kroll
The spiritual autobiography of a truly remarkable woman
and a history of the struggle for ordination in the Church of
England.
Paperback: 978-1-78279-804-0 ebook: 978-1-78279-805-7

The Quaker Way
A Rediscovery
Rex Ambler
Although fairly well known, Quakerism is not well
understood. The purpose of this book is to explain how
Quakerism works as a spiritual practice.
Paperback: 978-1-78099-657-8 ebook: 978-1-78099-658-5

Blue Sky God
The Evolution of Science and Christianity
Don MacGregor
Quantum consciousness, morphic fields and blue-sky thinking
about God and Jesus the Christ.
Paperback: 978-1-84694-937-1 ebook: 978-1-84694-938-8

Celtic Wheel of the Year
Tess Ward
An original and inspiring selection of prayers combining
Christian and Celtic Pagan traditions, and interweaving their
calendars into a single pattern of prayer for every morning and
night of the year.
Paperback: 978-1-90504-795-6

Christian Atheist
Belonging without Believing
Brian Mountford
Christian Atheists don't believe in God but miss him:
especially the transcendent beauty of his music, language,
ethics, and community.
Paperback: 978-1-84694-439-0 ebook: 978-1-84694-929-6

Compassion Or Apocalypse?
A Comprehensible Guide to the Thoughts of René Girard
James Warren
How René Girard changes the way we think about God and
the Bible, and its relevance for our apocalypse-threatened
world.
Paperback: 978-1-78279-073-0 ebook: 978-1-78279-072-3

Diary Of A Gay Priest
The Tightrope Walker
Rev. Dr. Malcolm Johnson
Full of anecdotes and amusing stories, but the Church is still a
dangerous place for a gay priest.
Paperback: 978-1-78279-002-0 ebook: 978-1-78099-999-9

Readers of ebooks can buy or view any of these bestsellers by
clicking on the live link in the title. Most titles are published
in paperback and as an ebook. Paperbacks are available in
traditional bookshops. Both print and ebook formats are
available online.

Find more titles and sign up to our readers' newsletter at
http://www.johnhuntpublishing.com/christianity Follow us on
Facebook at https://www.facebook.com/ChristianAlternative